Us for Them

Us for Them

Seeking Higher Ground in the Cultural Holy Wars

AUSTIN FISCHER

 CASCADE *Books* • Eugene, Oregon

US FOR THEM
Seeking Higher Ground in the Cultural Holy Wars

Copyright © 2024 Austin Fischer. All rights reserved. Except for brief quotations in critical publications or reviews, no part of this book may be reproduced in any manner without prior written permission from the publisher. Write: Permissions, Wipf and Stock Publishers, 199 W. 8th Ave., Suite 3, Eugene, OR 97401.

Cascade Books
An Imprint of Wipf and Stock Publishers
199 W. 8th Ave., Suite 3
Eugene, OR 97401

www.wipfandstock.com

PAPERBACK ISBN: 978-1-6667-7386-6
HARDCOVER ISBN: 978-1-6667-7387-3
EBOOK ISBN: 978-1-6667-7388-0

Cataloguing-in-Publication data:

Names: Fischer, Austin.

Title: Us for them : seeking higher ground in the cultural holy wars / Austin Fischer.

Description: Eugene, OR: Cascade Books, 2024 | Includes bibliographical references.

Identifiers: ISBN 978-1-6667-7386-6 (paperback) | ISBN 978-1-6667-7387-3 (hardcover) | ISBN 978-1-6667-7388-0 (ebook)

Subjects: LCSH: Christianity and culture | Religion and politics—United States | Christian life

Classification: BR115.C8 F48 2024 (paperback) | BR115.C8 (ebook)

03/29/24

All Scripture quotations, unless otherwise indicated, are taken from the NEW AMERICAN STANDARD BIBLE, Copyright 1960, 1962, 1963, 1968, 1971, 1972, 1973, 1975, 1977, 1995 by The Lockman Foundation. Used by permission.

To Quinn and Vista

"At such times it becomes even more urgent to try to strengthen the unity that is the church's fundamental vocation. Such is the commandment and prayer of the Lord: that we may be one as the Father and the Son are one with each other and in us, in a unity that we must live out while not withdrawing from a world in which the forces of evil tend to divide us. . . . This communion—common union—is at once a gift of God and a test set for us."

—Gustavo Gutiérrez, *A Theology of Liberation*

Contents

	Acknowledgments	ix
1	Justice + Friendship: An Invitation to ~~Middle~~ Higher Ground	1
2	Cats Must Also Fail: A Brief History of a Long History of Hate	20
3	The Coddling of the American Church: How the Big Sort Creates Communities of Spite, Sameness, and Sedentary Faith	32
4	The Day of Small Things: Learning to Think Little	45
5	Clashing Victimocracies: We (Not They) Are Causing the Crisis	60
6	Righteousness Porn: So You Think You're a Prophet?	79
7	Conservative and Progressive: A Better Story Together	88
8	Wendell Berry Would Like a Word: An Imaginary but Real Conversation Between an Old, White Farmer and a Young, Progressive Pastor on Trump, Whiteness, Friendship, Exaggeration, Anger, and the Unsettling of America	102
9	Twenty-Six Names: Are *You* Better than *Them*?	124
	Endnotes	137
	Bibliography	145

Acknowledgments

We mocked the culture wars of our parents. We shook our heads in disbelief at their desire to make America "great" again, cringed at their denial of systemic injustice, lovingly and condescendingly laughed at their nostalgia for something like Christian nationalism. And while I doubt many of us will ever fully agree with previous generations on these issues, it has become clear our problem was not with culture wars per se, but with what side our parents were on. For we, the mockers of our parents' culture warring, are apparently culture warriors too—we've just swapped banners. At least that was the conclusion I came to in the summer of 2020.

This book is the product of trying to sort out what Christian faith might say, not so much about all the specific issues in the conservative versus progressive culture wars of late western modernity, but about the culture war spirit more generally. It was humbling to write because it exposed how determined my identity had become by antagonistic contempt for those who disagreed with me on modern social issues. It exposed how much *I needed enemies*.

I have been at Vista Community Church for over a decade. It is an imperfect but wonderful place, filled with imperfect but wonderful people. I am grateful to get to belong there, and this book is a small gift, given in the hopes it might help Vista become a more just and friendly place as we await the full arrival of God's fierce, friendly justice. Any spillover is welcome but a secondary aspiration because books written for no one in particular are books written for no one.

Thanks to my family. We all come from broken families but our brokenness has always been an occasion for grace and gratitude. I doubt my children will always agree with everything in this book (I doubt I will

Acknowledgments

always agree with everything in this book!), but I hope it is a testimony to their dad's stubborn attempt to not make Christianity up.

Thanks again to Nate Hansen for helping me write like myself, but better. Thanks to Cascade Books for allowing me to write for them again. Thanks to Thomas Crosby Supper Club.

1

Justice + Friendship
An Invitation to ~~Middle~~ Higher Ground

I ONCE PREACHED AS fine a sermon on racism as an affluent white man can preach. Or so I thought. In retrospect, it was flawed. I ended the sermon with a true and beautiful story, but it probably wasn't mine to tell.

A white female police officer up the road in Dallas had killed Botham Jean, a twenty-six-year-old black man who was an accountant at PricewaterhouseCoopers. Jean was minding his own business in his own apartment when the officer, fresh off a long shift and absent her full wits, walked into his apartment thinking it was hers. Mistaking him for a burglar, she shot him. She was convicted of murder. During the sentencing, Jean's younger brother spoke, and he spoke forgiveness, going so far as to stand up, walk over to her, and embrace her.

I make no apologies for finding the story beautiful and instructive, but truth is always situated in time and space, which means aspiring truth-tellers must be sensitive to the temporal and spatial context. For various reasons, that true and beautiful story told *then* by *me* was not fitting. In the context of my actual church, almost the only context of which I am qualified to speak, it was a premature call for forgiveness, reconciliation, and unity. I know this because it was received that way by a black couple in my church, whom I dearly love, and I trust their judgement. But the sermon had more than one flaw.

Attempting to explain systemic racism, I had employed Harvard's famous Implicit Association Test, perhaps the most influential social psychology test. It measures our cognitive "reflexes" when shown various pictures, especially pictures of white and black people, and almost always delivers the humiliating news that you have pro-white and anti-black associations, which is to say, that you are at least a little bit racist. Living in a white supremacist culture, we all cultivate a baseline preference for whiteness, which manifests itself all the time in everything. Instead of denying it, all white people should simply admit they are at least a little racist and then commit themselves to the hard work of reparation and racial justice. So the argument goes.

A few days later, I was confronted by another parishioner with an objection to the sermon, but his objection cut the other way. He questioned how Harvard's high and holy racism test could measure, with such speed and certainty, what it claimed to measure. I found it amusing this non-college educated white conservative had the chutzpah to call Harvard to account, but mostly I found it tragic this racist white man couldn't just accept that he was racist. I was nice as I could be to someone I understood as an unintentional but unrepentant racist, but I ultimately gave him the dismissal he surely deserved.

A few months later, I was shocked to learn Harvard's world-famous Implicit Association Test was "problematic," which meant there was good reason to believe it greatly exaggerated its ability to measure bias. At risk of understatement, it is unclear if millisecond differences in reaction time to pictures of white and black people is evidence of racial bias, but the entire test is built upon the premise that it is, though no proof is or ever could be offered in support of this premise.[1] The flaw is so obvious it is painful to speak aloud.

Given that the test was not very good at doing the thing it allegedly did with mathematical precision, one might reasonably conclude the test was, as we would say it in central Texas, BS. The conclusion I drew was not that racial bias was not real (it obviously is), but that with the best of intentions I, and apparently many others, had become so ideologically gullible that I couldn't smell the BS when I was up to my knees in it.

I later found the presumed white conservative racist and let him know that while he may yet be a little bit racist, Harvard's little test could not prove it. To my surprise he agreed he probably harbored some racial bias, further agreed with the aforementioned black couple who felt Botham Jean's story was not mine to tell at that time and place, and simply wanted his pastor to be a little more thoughtful when dealing with such weighty matters. This book is an attempt to speak into that request.

UP!

God cannot be spoken well with a single word. We need at least two words to speak God well.

Scripture is our teacher: gospel and law, love and wrath, absolution and judgment, charity and severity, forgiveness and justice, order and revolution, revelation and mystery. Speaking of God faithfully requires speaking both words; the *yes* and the *no*. Truth emerges from the tension. Truth might be a middle ground, but often it is not. Truth is a summons to holier, higher ground.

But we like speaking God with a single word. It is easier, leaving us surer of ourselves. Every theological and ideological tribe has its pet words and anathemas, words it loves and words it loathes. But these one-word monologues are theological slander.

Solomon knew this: "It is good that you grasp one thing and also not let go of the other; for the one who fears God comes forth with both of them" (Eccl 7:18). We might even venture that, in many cases, we either come forth with both of them, or we come forth with neither.

Karl Barth concurred. His *Church Dogmatics* is the most consequential theological work of the modern era, and an audacious performance of theological dialectics. He doesn't spend thousands of pages resolving theology's tensions; he spends thousands of pages *performing* them. Truth emerges as the tensions are performed, not resolved.

Hegel, a philosopher of no small consequence, did something similar. He called it *aufhenbung*. The word's basic associative picture is lifting something from a lower to higher place. It has a double meaning of negation and affirmation. Moments of true understanding, of revelation, consist of a movement wherein something is partly denied, partly affirmed, but ultimately transcended.

The vertical move—that's what Charles Taylor calls it.[2] Locked in flat, horizontal, zero-sum, right-versus-left dilemmas, we need a transcendent tap on the head and a summons up. Jesus was fond of the vertical move.

Do we pay taxes to Caesar, or not?
Render Caesar's things to Caesar and God's to God.
Upon arriving in heaven, which of the seven brothers will own a woman to whom they were all married?
Patriarchy is not a factor in the politics of heaven.
Who sinned: the blind man or his parents?
Neither—move while I heal him.

Will you make my brother split the inheritance with me?
Once upon a time there was a rich fool.
Right or left or middle?
Up!

Solomon's both, Barth's dialectics, Hegel's *aufhenbung*, and Christ's vexing verticality were virtuoso performances of truth emerging through tension. Because we don't need assault or arbitration; we need ascension. What follows is no such virtuosity, but an attempt to speak well about the shape of Christian faithfulness in modernity by refusing to speak of God with a single word. More specifically, what follows is an attempt to speak well of God and transcend the cultural tug-of-war that fashions itself as a holy war by speaking two words well: justice and friendship.

THE MIRROR IS SHATTERED

We have never not been divided. There is no golden age of solidarity to which we can return, no Camelot of perfect harmony beckoning from the mists of an earlier, more benign time. Those who opine the acrimonious state of modern culture and politics forget that in the nineteenth century it was not unusual for politicians to sort their differences by dueling—a euphemism for standing a few feet apart and shooting one another. A nasty tweet can maim, but a tiny lead ball rifled into your torso at a thousand feet per second can, well, actually maim. Similarly, politicians got along much better in the mid-twentieth century, and while they were getting along civil rights activists were being beaten to death in the streets.

So, while modern culture is quarrelsome and divisive, culture has always been quarrelsome and divisive. Water is wet, the sky is blue, people quarrel, and people quarrelling does not mean the sky is falling.

And yet while not necessarily uniquely divided, we are divided in unique ways, and our divisions merit scrutiny. Rabbi Jonathan Sacks calls it *cultural climate change*, and it's a phenomenon we'll gradually explore.[3] But far more importantly, as Christians, we are obligated to find our (modern American, but especially modern *Christian*) divisiveness not merely personally annoying or socially counterproductive or emotionally exhausting or manifestly uncivilized but *sinful*.

This claim begs for pitiless interrogation, and it's not a claim I'm particularly fond of, but it's a claim Christian faith plainly imposes upon its adherents. And all sorts of qualifications and amplifications must and will follow, but if those qualifications and amplifications have taken the teeth out of the claim, then the faith has been betrayed and the gospel rendered unbelievable. Jesus himself says as much:

> I do not ask on behalf of these alone, but for those also who believe in Me through their word; that they may all be one; even as You, Father, are in Me and I in You, that they may also be in Us, so that the world may believe that You sent Me. The glory which You have given Me I have given to them, that they may be one, just as We are one; I in them and You in Me, that they may be perfected in unity, so that the world may know that You sent Me, and loved them, even as You have loved Me. (John 17:20–23)

What would it take for the world to believe God sent Jesus? A sign in the sky? A Christian takeover of world governments? Justice raining down from the heavens? The perfect rational argument for the existence of God?

According to Jesus, the unity of his disciples is determinative of the world's capacity to believe God sent him, meaning our unity helps make the gospel believable—conversely, this means our disunity makes the gospel *unbelievable*. Our disunity is a stumbling block upon which the world cannot help but trip, and woe to those who are stumbling blocks. In the sober but lucid words of Gerhard Lohfink, "No one has ever seen God. . . . What can be seen is only the Church. If it is no longer one, but divided, the world can only indistinctly behold the mystery of Christ. The mirror is shattered. The division of the people of God makes it almost impossible for the world to believe."[4]

Because how is the world to believe Jesus of Nazareth is powerful enough to destroy the barrier separating God from humanity and life from death when he is incapable of destroying the intramural barriers separating Catholics and Baptists or conservative and progressive Christians?

Channeling Jesus in John 17, Saint Paul goes so far as to say our seditious reflexes are "unworthy" of our calling, no matter how skillful we justify them to ourselves:

> Therefore I, the prisoner of the Lord, implore you to walk in a manner worthy of the calling with which you have been called, with all humility and gentleness, with patience, showing tolerance for one another in love, being diligent to preserve the unity of the Spirit in the bond of peace. There is one body and one Spirit, just as also you were called in one hope of your calling; one Lord, one faith, one baptism, one God and Father of all who is over all and through all and in all. (Eph 4:1–6)

But such calls for unity deserve ruthless scrutiny and careful refining, lest, as bell hooks observes, dissenting voices "be silenced by the collective demand for harmony."[5] Rowan Williams has said this well: "The premature embrace of harmony turns out to be an act of violence in its own way."[6]

BUT THERE IS NO PEACE

Why, for example, are most meetings worthless? Because nothing happens—no one says what they think because that would create conflict. Most meetings are like a trip to the zoo—carefully controlled, leisurely strolls where nothing happens, and nothing is at stake. There is no risk, no danger, no chance of a brutish encounter. Perhaps the lion will roar behind his steel bars and concrete fortress, and we'll look at the king of the jungle, toddler in tow and popcorn in hand, telling ourselves we're walking on the wild side.

Priya Parker is an expert on meetings. She's discovered that meetings need risk and healthy conflict if they are to be productive, and, consequently, "most of our gatherings suffer from unhealthy peace, not unhealthy conflict."[7] And what is true of meetings in dull, fluorescently sedated conference rooms is true of modern life writ large—we suffer from unhealthy peace just as much as we suffer from unhealthy conflict. An old Jewish prophet agrees.

Around twenty-five hundred years ago, the city of Jerusalem was on the brink of destruction, but you wouldn't have known it. The economy was booming, the city was growing, leaders were encouraging citizens to take trips to Disney World. The only inconvenience was an obstinate prophet named Jeremiah who kept harassing everyone with doomsday proclamations of a looming judgment: things are not OK, the city reeks of injustice, and the wallpapered peace must be torn down!

> From the prophet even to the priest
> Everyone deals falsely.
> They have healed the brokenness of My people superficially,
> Saying, "Peace, peace,"
> But there is no peace. (Jer 6:13–14)

The world has always been filled with phony prophets peddling wallpapered peace. (I do not think I am one, but few phony prophets think they're phony.) Relative to most of the world, I am a very powerful and privileged person, and powerful and privileged people have a vested interest in keeping the peace because that typically means preserving the status quo. And preserving the status quo typically means preserving my power and privilege. What I call *peace*, others might call *oppression*.

THE WHITE MODERATE

At the close of the twentieth century, a Gallup poll found that Americans admired Martin Luther King Jr. more than any human of that century except for Mother Teresa. Yet at the time of King's death, 75 percent of Americans *disapproved* of him.[8] And as much as we like to think we would have been included in that approving 25 percent, there's at least a 75 percent chance we're wrong. I was certainly wrong.

A few years back, I was asked to speak at a MLK Day rally in my city, so I did what white pastors do when extended such invitations—hastily appropriated a few uplifting King quotes. But in my brazen pillaging of King's work, I made the fortuitous mistake of *actually reading King*, and suddenly understood why I would have disapproved of him: he would have disapproved of me.

In his often-cited but (it would seem) rarely understood "Letter from Birmingham Jail," King is responding to a group of well-meaning white pastors generally sympathetic to his desire for racial justice but critical of his methods. They agreed racial injustice was wrong but felt King's methods were too aggressive. They wanted justice but not at the expense of peace. Few things have complicated my life more than King's reply:

> I must make a confession to you, my Christian brothers. I must confess that over the past few years I have been gravely disappointed with the white moderate. I have almost reached the regrettable conclusion that the Negro's great stumbling block in his stride toward freedom is not the Ku Klux Klanner, but the white moderate, who is more devoted to "order" than to justice. . . . Shallow understanding from people of good will is more frustrating than absolute misunderstanding from people of ill will. Lukewarm acceptance is much more bewildering than outright rejection.[9]

On June 7, 1998, James Byrd accepted a ride from an acquaintance and two other men, but instead of taking Byrd home, the three white men took him to a remote county road, beat him, and tied him to the back of their truck, dragging him for three miles. Forensics suggest Byrd was alive and conscious for most of the dragging, right up to the moment he hit a culvert and his head was severed. His murderers dumped his shattered body in front of an African American church and then drove off to a barbeque.

This happened an hour from my house when I was twelve years old, and it was the first time I remember feeling outright moral rage. I remember wanting those three white men to die. I remember the surge of moral superiority. But here was the most admired black man in world history calling me, a white moderate, a greater racial stumbling block than a Ku Klux Klanner.

Why? Because I am more devoted to order than justice.

JUSTICE & FRIENDSHIP—PLAYING THE TENSION

Christianity is a religion of justice and friendship, and uniquely so. While the world's other great religions typically tilt toward one or the other, Christianity has stubbornly embraced both. The same God who thunders judgment from the Jewish prophets pronounces pardon upon his executioners *as they are executing him*, prior to any gesture of penance.

> Like a cage full of birds,
> So their houses are full of deceit;
> Therefore they have become great and rich.
> They are fat, they are sleek,
> They also excel in deeds of wickedness;
> They do not plead the cause,
> The cause of the orphan, that they may prosper;
> And they do not defend the rights of the poor.
> "Shall I not punish these people?"
> Declares the Lord.
> "On a nation such as this
> Shall I not avenge Myself?" (Jer 5:27–29)

"Father, forgive them; for they do not know what they are doing."
(Luke 23:34)

The stubborn embrace of justice and friendship means Christianity is a religion singularly at odds with itself. Progressive Christians who loathe to speak of God's judgment upon sinners have no problem calling down fire from heaven upon fundamentalist evangelicals who support cruel social policies that target minorities and immigrants. Conservative Christians who speak fondly and frequently of God's judgment upon individual sinners get strangely peaceable and passive when asked how that judgment translates into the crooked social structures that plague our fallen world (unless we're talking about abortion). But this isn't necessarily intentional duplicity or the deliberate practice of bad faith—it's the struggle to negotiate Christianity's foundational tension.

This tension plays out in infinite variations on the basic theme of justice and friendship and manifests a proposal: instead of trying to *resolve* the tension, let's follow the lead of maestros like Solomon, Barth, Hegel, Taylor, Mandela, Tutu, Christ, and *play* it. Let's stop trying to win the newest season of the culture war, and let's start jamming together. Let's trade bars, reciprocate riffs, symphonize instead of solo. Not because the stakes aren't high, but because they are. Let's play the tension so the Spirit has space to synthesize unexpected melodies much more interesting than the monotone droning we make on our own.

Some tensions make noise—fingernails scraping a chalkboard, partisans shrieking talking-point screeds at one another, wannabe Christian influencers reciprocating Twitter insults. Such tensions are a waste and distraction, actively damaging to the common good. We should doggedly rid ourselves of such tensions; we should resolve them.

But not all tensions make noise; some make music—the strings on a guitar, the compressed air in a saxophone, the activist philosophies of Malcom X and MLK. These tensions produce notes and harmonies that cannot exist without friction. In ridding ourselves of noisy, unnecessary tensions, we must be careful lest we also slacken and thus lose those that fill our world with joyful music. If we prioritize justice over friendship or friendship over justice, we will be left with neither justice nor friendship—we will be left with a world of noise or silence but no music.

We inhabit a particular cultural moment where the tension between justice and friendship is so acute it feels unbearable, which has resulted in well-meaning but misguided attempts to *resolve* it. In American Christianity, this has carved out a few predictable ruts. Progressives accuse conservatives of preserving systems of oppression and injustice under the auspices of championing traditional values and biblical orthodoxy. Bluntly, progressives don't think conservatives are able or willing to understand systemic injustice because conservatives are too deeply vested in preserving the injustice they call order, the oppression they call peace. Conservatives are quick to call for unity and friendship, but slow to work for justice.

Meanwhile, conservatives accuse progressives of flattening the faith into a strictly horizontal vision of human flourishing marked by modernity's moral trinity: removing limits to "freedom," fighting exclusion, and mitigating suffering. Bluntly, conservatives think progressives are often more progressive than distinctively Christian, with progressive Christianity regularly serving as the antechamber to agnostic humanism or tepid deism. To the degree Christianity is useful for progressive social causes, progressives are happy to use Christianity, but are they willing to submit to it?

The middle of the road is marked by a rut no less dangerous by being in the middle—the exhausted or oblivious apolitical "moderates" who find politics distracting and just want everyone to get along. Progressives accuse them of a dereliction of social duty and a tacit endorsement of injustice. Conservatives accuse them of naively bowing out of an ideological culture war where the future of the faith (and, more importantly, the Christian nation) is at stake. If conservatives and progressives seek to remove Christianity's justice/friendship tension by removing one or the other, apolitical moderates remove it by removing both and turning Jesus into the equivalent of the modern spiritual influencer who inspires us with banal spiritual goodwill. This is the pusillanimous "Swiss neutrality" that Karl Barth mocked during World War II when Swiss authorities expected people "to act as though we saw no difference between . . . Hitler and Churchill."[10]

There are people of genuine faith on all sides, each declaring certain truths. Conservatives are not crying wolf by claiming our "secular age" is more anti-religious than objective, nor are they hysterical for intuiting progressives are overly accommodating to the prevailing winds of secular culture. And yet, progressives are right in asserting conservative Christians often mistake past cultural norms (and especially past white cultural norms) for orthodox Christian faith, and thus end up defending forms of privilege and supremacy that masquerade as the faith of Abraham, Isaac, and Jacob. And moderates, apolitical or otherwise, aren't rubes for claiming something is amiss in the climate shaping modern political identity.

But here's the rub: the divisive ruts we're stuck in, both inside and outside the church, cannot be escaped by anyone "winning." Because if progressives, conservatives, or moderates "win" the ideological culture war, we lose the tension that creates Christianity's oddly joyful and just music.

Speaking about a situation far afield on the surface but sharing a common root, Wendell Berry tells a story about the defenders of the coyote and the defenders of the sheep. In the world of ecological ethics, coyote loyalists feel nature should be left as wild as possible, and the coyote thus free to wreak whatever havoc nature naturally allows. This will mean many dead sheep, but so be it. These defenders of the coyote are opposed by the defenders of the sheep: sheep ranchers who find coyotes a menace and want to do away with both them and their defenders. Who is right? Who should win?

Berry notes that once we push past the propaganda, we discern both camps have authentic concerns and complaints because we need a world hospitable to the flourishing of both coyotes and sheep since "neither will prosper in a world totally unfit for the other." And this battle between coyotes and sheep is just one example of a conflict in which someone (anyone) "winning" is the worst possible outcome:

> It is a dangerous mistake, I think, for either side to pursue such a quarrel on the assumption that victory would be a desirable result.... This sort of conflict, then, does not suggest the possibility of victory so much as it suggests the possibility of a compromise—some kind of peace, even an alliance, between the domestic and the wild.[11]

Over the beautiful but brutal course of human history, one wonders how much we've lost due to the deluded assumption that victory was always the goal. Abraham Lincoln wondered the same. At the apex of the Civil War, he wrote himself a private note with a scandalous sentence: "In the present Civil War it is quite possible that God's purpose is something different from the purpose of either party..."[12]

Here's a man of enormous moral conviction, conducting a horrific war he finds awful but necessary, wagering millions of lives (including his own) on his conviction, but nevertheless conceding it's quite possible his view on the conflict is not God's view on the conflict. He acts decisively and, he believes, righteously, but knows God might well be up to something beyond the horizons of even his great intellect. As a result, he does not demonize his opponents.

A year later, war still raging, he dared to offer a proclamation in which he implored *all* Americans to express "humble penitence for our national perverseness and disobedience."[13] Instead of rallying his side against the other with the spectacle of a spite-filled frenzy, Lincoln asks people he is also asking to kill each other to see each other as fallen but beloved sons of the eternal God. He invites enemy combatants to confess their sins to one another. He invites a people at war to entertain the possibility even their brutal conflict is subservient to a larger mission to defeat victory as we have always known it.

Shifting the focus from coyotes, sheep, and the Civil War, and back to the uncivil wars demanding to define modern culture, I am not suggesting everyone gets a participation trophy. All options are not always equal. But I am suggesting many of our tensions are complementary instead of contradictory, better perceived as duets than duels, and thus it is foolish to keep proceeding on the assumption that victory is always desirable. Many times it is not. Many times your victory or my victory means *our* loss. As Berry has also said, "the way to prevent disagreements from becoming destructive is to seek clarity rather than victory."[14]

Progressives, conservatives, and moderates need each other, and the common good seems best served through their collaboration and not their warfare. So I am suggesting that we're wasting time and energy seeking victory instead of clarity, wasting time and energy trying to defeat them and resolve the tension instead of collaborating with them to play the tension.

Returning to the necessary but necessarily interrogated claim made earlier, I am also suggesting something more extreme—whether or not we can learn from each other (and we can), and whether or not our collaboration best serves the common good (and it does), and regardless any other pragmatic consideration, our Lord has commanded us to be *for* each other. Jesus' brother is right: "the anger of man cannot accomplish God's justice." There's no cause so righteous it gives you permission to have enemies you don't love.

SYSTEMIC FRIENDSHIP

In the closing moments of World War II, Karl Barth found himself in an odd position. For he was German but had also been one of the most rigorous opponents of Nazism, and now that the Nazi defeat was certain there was deep confusion about what Germany needed. Barth's answer was that while Germany needed justice, they also needed friends—"friends in spite of everything." And in a lecture called "The Germans and Us," he imagined what Jesus might say to the Germans by speaking of justice and friendship:

> Come to me you unlovely creatures, you wicked Hitler youth and Hitler girls, you brutal SS soldiers, you evil Gestapo blackguards, you sorry compromisers and collaborationists, you sheep who now have run so patiently and so dumbly for so long behind your so-called leader! Come to me, you guilty ones and you connivers! Now you can and must see what your actions are really worth! Come to me!

> I know you well, but I do not ask who you are and what you have done. I can only see that you are finished, and for good or ill you must begin again. I will refresh you. Now I will begin again with you from scratch.... I am for you! I am your friend![15]

I don't know if this is exactly what Jesus would have said, but it does sound something like something Jesus might say.

One of my heroes is a man named Bennie Walsh—he's a security guard at the local high school and president of the NAACP branch in our city. Bennie shoulders a heavy load for many people and is a relational ambassador between many groups. He advocates for the equality and advancement of minorities in our city, he regularly meets with our police chief, and he calls our Republican state representative a good friend. Few could shoulder such a load well, but Bennie manages it with dignity and warmth.

I have seen Bennie have a tough but friendly conversation with the police chief, and then walk over and hug the parents of a child who had recently been killed by a police officer. He is a man working for justice and friendship. I once heard someone ask him how he managed to have so many friendships with so many kinds of people. "Well, it's not easy," he said, "but it is simple: I make myself friendly to everybody. Jesus told me to do it."

Friendship has come under fire in recent years, and understandably so. Many will find my pairing of justice and friendship odd, perhaps a category mistake—perhaps a serious one. What has Athens to do with Jerusalem? For at times friendship is the name given to unjust compromise. It has become standard to observe that conservatives are often personally friendly to minorities all the while endorsing social norms that preserve minority oppression (the white evangelical who is friendly with the black family who has a son on his son's football team but mainlines FOX News every night and is convinced black people only vote Democrat because they've been brainwashed). Personal friendships cannot single-handedly solve our systemic problems, but our systemic problems cannot be solved without friendship.

In a deceptively perceptive sentence, Stanley Hauerwas has suggested modern society is stranded in a partisan lagoon because it has pursued justice at all costs and neglected political friendship: "Friendship has been abandoned in favor of trying to make justice the primary political virtue."[16]

No justice, no peace. Absolutely! But no friendship, no justice. Why? Because people who hate each other cannot agree on justice because they cannot agree on truth because victory is more important than communion.

Miroslav Volf agrees: "To agree on justice . . . you must want more than justice; you must want embrace. There can be no justice without the will to embrace."[17]

This does not seem debatable. You can walk into a negotiation loaded with unimpeachable facts and steel explanations, but if the person sitting across the table hates you or thinks you hate them, you probably couldn't agree on anything of consequence if your lives depended on it. Further elaborating, Volf says,

> To agree on justice you need to make space in yourself for the perspective of the other, and in order to make space, you need to want to embrace the other. If you insist that others do not belong to you and you to them, that their perspective should not muddle yours, you will have your justice and they will have theirs; your justices will clash and there will be no justice *between* you. The knowledge of justice depends on the will to embrace.[18]

Willie James Jennings teaches systematic theology and Africana studies at Yale. He has explored this delicate territory better than most, arguing modern Western notions of friendship are the bastardized children of colonialism and capitalism wherein friendship is primarily conceived as a personal choice wherein two individuals who do not need each other decide to share, care, and connect. And while acknowledging such individualistic and voluntarist visions of friendship come bearing certain truths, Jennings believes all friendship occurs on a deeper social fabric that must be seen, understood, and transformed.[19]

Writing specifically of the ideological trench warfare surrounding justice that's occurring in higher education, Jennings prophesies only a mounting body count because the goal of modern ideological combat is critique and not communion, and while critique is an indispensable means it's an unworthy end: "We forget that critique itself is being overturned, turned right side up within the new purpose of life together. Critique must aim at communion. . . . [We] make a terrible mistake when [we] forget communion is the point."[20]

True communion requires critique, but critique must be motivated by the desire for communion, otherwise our critique is not Christian, whatever else it may be.

Rowan Williams concurs from a contemplative angle, advocating for a contemplative politics motivated by the pursuit of sustainable justice and not the spasms of ideology. A contemplative politics is one that "seeks to make room for the narrative of the other; one that does not begin by attempting to absorb this narrative into itself, and thus is willing to learn how it is itself seen and understood."[21] Sounds pleasant enough. But making room for the narrative of the other proves wickedly difficult because it requires something that feels wicked to cultural holy warriors: we must distance ourselves from our political commitments.

Progressives will likely hear this as a privileged counsel of oppressive passive-ism. Conservatives will likely hear this as a naïve counsel of cowardly nicety. But Williams contends that such hearings expose the futility of pursuing the victory of holy-war justice instead of the communion of sustainable justice: "To say that we must learn to distance ourselves from our commitments in politics in order to arrive at both justice and love is at first sight a bizarre recommendation, suggesting a corrosive indifferentism. But the distance involved is not a refusal of commitment; it has rather to do with what it is that we are committed *to*."[22]

And what we must be *ultimately* committed to is not victory—what we must be ultimately committed to is each other. For only if our commitment to each other is more ultimate than our commitment to victory will we ceaselessly pursue a justice that is sustainable because sustained by the contemplative capacity to make room for the other that we might, more simply, call friendship.

The father of Latin American liberation theology, Gustavo Gutierrez, agrees in the updated introduction to his classic work, *A Theology of Liberation*, affirming that liberation is a means to friendship, just as friendship is the means to liberation. For the liberation from sin that is friendship is the only thing that "gets to the very source of social injustice and other forms of human oppression . . ."[23]

So rather than abandoning friendship in the name of justice, we are better served transposing friendship into a systemic key. Systemic injustice plagues our world, but so does systemic hostility, and systemic hostility makes systemic justice impossible because it makes both truth and communion impossible. This brings us to the friendly but firm argument at the center of this book: Jesus has commanded the church to be a place of *systemic justice and systemic friendship*, a space where the hostilities that make justice, peace, and communion impossible are exposed, diagnosed, and healed. Because not only is friendship not irrelevant to the pursuit of justice, and not only is justice not irrelevant to the pursuit of friendship, but there is no justice or friendship without justice and friendship.

GOD'S JOYFUL JUSTICE

In February 2016, Hillary Clinton stood in Harlem giving a speech about race and became the first major-party candidate to use the term "systemic racism" in a public address.[24] Since then, the term has become a popular explanation of how racialized structures embedded in American culture perpetuate the oppression of minorities, but these structures are mostly unnoticed precisely because they are so ubiquitous. We struggle to see the systemic oppression in our educational, economic, and judicial systems because it is all we can see, and when something is all we can see it becomes especially hard to see—just as a fish can't "see" water because water is all a fish can see.

Without diminishing the reality of systemic racism and injustice, we could benefit from applying the insights we've gleaned in our grappling with them to create a broader vision. We are caught up in habits and systems that normalize injustice, but we're also caught up in habits and systems that normalize hostility, and injustice and hostility are destructively reinforcing forces. They cannot be solved separately. Hostility can achieve victories, but it cannot achieve justice. And that's where systemic friendship comes in—not as a rebuttal to the pursuit of systemic justice, but rather as a collaborator.

Systemic friendship is a posture of the heart—the will to embrace, the desire for communion. It is created and sustained by and as a culture—an environment of habits, practices, systems, and stories that normalizes a relentless commitment to the good of others. It normalizes a posture of "for" instead of "against." It does not replace or neuter the pursuit of justice but rather pursues Christian justice, a justice whose form is the crucifixion of the son of God and the justification of the ungodly.

Because is justice an end in itself? Surely that depends on what we mean by justice.[25]

In common parlance, justice is mostly synonymous with fairness—justice is everyone getting what they deserve. But force the concept into practice, and justice usually means we get what we deserve when we deserve good but not when we deserve bad, and everyone else gets what we think they deserve. We should not be shocked this hasn't worked out well. If this is or anything like it is what justice means, no, justice is not an end in itself. In fact, the crucifixion expresses God's commitment to give everyone what they *don't* deserve: grace. Litigious objectivity is not one of God's attributes—thanks be to God!

Miroslav Volf elaborates on his aforementioned claim that "justice requires the will to embrace" like this: "There is a profound injustice about the God of the biblical tradition. It is called grace. . . . If we want the God of the prophets and the God of Jesus Christ, we will have to put up with the injustice of God's grace—and rethink the concept of justice."[26]

Provocative in the early 1990s and more so now, Hauerwas' essay "The Politics of Justice: Why Justice is a Bad Idea for Christians" explores the growing centrality of justice in modern Christianity, for "if there is anything Christians agree about today it is that our faith is one that does justice."[27] Atoning for overly spiritualized forms of Christianity that were so heavenly minded they were no earthly good, many of us now seek a spirituality with teeth and not wings, a faith whose salvation is social and political and not merely spiritual. This is a welcome and wonderful development.

The problem, as Hauerwas (with a nod to Alasdair MacIntyre) sees it, is that modern people have vastly overestimated our ability to agree on what constitutes justice. Whose justice? It's simply not the case that so long as we're "reasonable" we'll agree on justice. As a result, "appeals to justice have simply gotten out of hand . . . [and] . . . the current emphasis on justice and rights as the primary norms guiding the social witness of Christians is in fact a mistake."[28]

Indeed. The call for justice has never been louder, yet it's never been clearer that it's unclear we know exactly what we're calling for when we call for justice. So rather than being compliant modern citizens who allow our societies to sustain the lie that we all more or less agree on justice, Christians serve our societies best when we refuse "to continue the illusion that the larger social order knows what it is talking about when it calls for justice."[29]

Well before modernity had a name, Dostoyevsky prophesied that attempts to create a just order with reason *sans* Christ were doomed because no God = no sin = no justice:

> They hope to create a just order for themselves, but, having rejected Christ, they will end by drenching the earth with blood. . . . And were it not for Christ's covenant, they would annihilate one another down to the last two men on earth. And these last two, in their pride, would not be able to restrain each other either, so that the last would annihilate the next to last, and them himself as well.[30]

A bleak picture, but I'm not convinced he's wrong.

That said, we do not (and must not!) give up on justice. But we must recover a biblical sense of justice where the emphasis is not everyone getting what they deserve but everyone receiving mercy and experiencing communion. If we pursue justice first and at all costs, we will be left with an unfriendly justice that is not God's justice. If we pursue friendship first and at all costs, we will be left with an unjust friendship that is not God's friendship. But if we pursue justice and friendship concurrently and equally, we practice God's fierce, friendly justice.

God's justice is God's dogged commitment to defeat sin, suffering, oppression, injustice, and death, and set the world "right"—right having *nothing* to do with what we deserve and *everything* to do with God's mercy. This is no soft justice neutered by permissiveness but a severe justice utterly resolved to redound to the flourishing of all the sons and daughters of God. As Fleming Rutledge says, the justice and wrath of God can only be understood as "the unconditional love of God manifested against anything that would frustrate or destroy the designs of his love."[31] And *this* justice is indeed an end in itself because it is the joy of the kingdom. Another old Jewish prophet agrees:

> For You have been a defense for the helpless,
> A defense for the needy in his distress,
> A refuge from the storm, a shade from the heat;
> For the breath of the ruthless
> Is like a rain storm against a wall.
> Like heat in drought, You subdue the uproar of aliens;
> Like heat by the shadow of a cloud, the song of the ruthless is silenced.
> The Lord of hosts will prepare a lavish banquet for all people on this mountain;
> A banquet of aged wine, choice pieces with marrow,
> And refined, aged wine.
> And on this mountain He will swallow up the covering which is over all peoples,
> Even the veil which is stretched over all nations.
> He will swallow up death for all time,
> And the Lord God will wipe tears away from all faces.
> . . . .
> And it will be said in that day,
> "Behold, this is our God for whom we have waited that He might save us.
> This is the Lord for whom we have waited;
> Let us rejoice and be glad in His salvation." (Isa 25:4–9)

This is how the world ends and God's new world begins: injustice annihilated, hostility exterminated, the song of the ruthless silenced, and creation covered with the joyful justice of God. Even now, all things are being pulled toward *this* future—not a cold courtroom where all lobby for themselves and against others, but a cosmic party constituted by revelry without limit because God's justice has finally been done and will be forever and ever. Even now, all things are being pulled up into the elevation of the kingdom.

To say Jesus has commanded the church to be a place of systemic justice and friendship is to say the church is the space in time where the Spirit helps us practice God's future now. It is where God's joyful and just future patiently becomes present. It is where systemic hostility (us *versus* them) becomes systemic justice and friendship (us *for* them). It is where we speak justice *and* friendship, not justice *or* friendship. Because God cannot be spoken well with a single word.

2

Cats Must Also Fail
A Brief History of a Long History of Hate

NEFARIOUS GRINS UPON THEIR faces, two dogs in suits sit at a luxurious bar. One sips a martini, the other a pint of beer. Clearly, they have done well in life, but they are up to no good. One speaks, the other listens, and the conspiracy is divulged: "It's not enough that we succeed. Cats must also fail."

In two sentences and a few brush strokes, Leo Cullum's famous *New Yorker* cartoon says definitively what we all sense so deeply: we love to hate. Cats versus dogs, Democrats versus Republicans, conservatives versus progressives, working versus stay-at-home moms, Lakers versus Celtics, Edison versus Tesla, Hatfields versus McCoys—we blush admitting it because it's impolite to say out loud, but the friction of a fight warms our hearts. Antagonism energizes us. Or as Will Blythe says it in the indisputably perfect title of his book exploring the Duke/North Carolina basketball rivalry, *To Hate Like This Is to Be Happy Forever.*[32]

To hate like this is to be happy forever—who could deny it's true? A few hundred years before Christ, a philosopher named Diogenes Laertius is alleged to have delightfully defined hate as "a growing or lasting desire or craving that it should go ill with somebody." And once you've tasted it, the craving is not easily satiated. Certainly, no reasonable person could deny *schadenfreude* (literally "harm + joy") is both the most delightful word in the German language and a high like no other. Because winning is nice, but watching your enemy fail is bliss. Case in point, Beto O'Rourke.

It had been almost thirty years since Texas had elected a Democratic senator, but in 2018 O'Rourke gave incumbent Republican senator Ted Cruz an unexpected scare. Though he was fairly anonymous and far from a political virtuoso, O'Rourke raised more money than anyone in American history for a Senate race and received the most votes ever cast for a Democrat in Texas history. But, most importantly, Beyoncé endorsed him and posted a photo of herself wearing a Beto hat on Election Day! In the end, he narrowly lost to Cruz, but his astonishingly competitive performance made him a sensation, such a sensation that he decided to run for president.

Alas, his presidential bid was not as sensational. He dropped out before the primaries, having received zero delegates, and, if Wikipedia is to be believed, one total vote.[33] We can't prove the lone vote was from his mother, but we'd be remiss to rule it out. How could this be? How could Beto almost defeat Ted Cruz, an incumbent Republican senator in a red state who himself had a much more successful failed bid for president in 2016, and then run for president and receive as many votes as you did? The answer: negative partisanship. As it turns out, Beto's momentum was less a result of exuberance for his candidacy and more a result of drafting off people's dislike for Ted Cruz, and Ted Cruz was a rather disliked fellow in liberal circles. Summarizing this case study and applying it to modern politics in general, Ezra Klein suggests:

> Nothing brings a group together like a common enemy. Remove the fury and fear . . . and watch the enthusiasm drain from your supporters. . . . The catalytic ingredient in [Beto's] Senate campaign was liberal loathing of Cruz, the thrill that he might be defeated. . . . This lesson is known by politicians the world over. You don't just need support. You need anger.[34]

My sports allegiance belongs to two teams—the Dallas Mavericks and Texas Longhorns. Both teams won championships during my young adulthood, and the primary spoil of those victories was *schadenfreude*, the rapturous glee that washed over me as I beheld the humiliation of LeBron James's diabolical mercenary dynasty (also known as the 2011 Miami Heat) and Pete Carroll's entitled and fraudulent West Coast evil empire (also known as the 2005 USC Trojans). Besides the birth of my children and probably my wedding, I have never been happier.

It's been suggested that stories were mankind's first true invention, and that seems right. So far as we know, we're the only creatures who tell stories, and our stories give us mastery: "Who tells the story creates the world."[35] The world is filled with stories, and the stories we tell ourselves about the world don't just *describe* but also *shape* the world, determining what happens and not merely describing what happens. Our stories are not passive but active and ambitious, self-fulfilling prophecies seeking to impose reality upon reality. And when one takes stock of the seemingly limitless variety of stories that populate our planet vying for mastery, one cannot help but notice most stories contract to the same simple plot: *us versus them*.

Travel our wild world far and wide—listen to the stories told in huts in primal Amazon rainforests, in the open office spaces of transparent Silicon Valley suites, on the felt boards of Southern Baptist Sunday school classrooms—and while there are differences in the details, the base narrative is the boilerplate monotony of *us versus them*.

But how did this story become the most powerful story we tell about ourselves? How did this story create the world? How did the most important thing about *you* become *them*? This brings us to a brief history of the long history of hate.

PART ONE: THE EIGHTH DAY

In 1849, a man dug up seven clay tablets, and scribbled across them was the oldest story in the history of the world. Known as the *Enuma Elish*, it was an ancient Babylonian creation story that first told the tale of us versus them.

In the beginning, there were two primeval gods, Apsu and Tiamat. These primeval gods then created the second-generation gods, a decision they quickly regretted because the second gods (like all offspring) were a noisy, boisterous brood, so the primeval gods decided to kill their progeny. A battle of the gods ensued, ending when Marduk, the strongest of the young gods, defeated Tiamat and ripped her dead carcass into two halves, one of which he used to make the heavens and the other the earth. According to the oldest story ever told, the heavens and the earth are the two halves of a murdered god's dismembered carcass. According to the oldest story ever told, the cosmos itself is a monument to hostility.

In the Genesis creation story, the hostility is delayed, but only until "the eighth day." God creates for six days, rests on the seventh, and then on the eighth day we hear the first hiss of hostility.

Eden is brimming with benevolence, and Adam and Eve haven't a worry—they are the good creatures in the good garden of a good God. But how good is God? Good enough to trust unreservedly? When the serpent (or as he will become known upon later reflection, *Satan*) strikes up a conversation with Eve, he does so as the original antagonist, provoking subtle mistrust and malice. The permissive largesse of God's invitation to eat from every tree of the garden except for one (Gen 2:16–17) is inverted as the serpent deliberately misquotes God's command, emphasizing the prohibition: "Did God really tell you not to eat from any tree of the garden?" (Gen 3:1). Eve corrects the serpent, but the enmity has been planted, and as the conversation unfolds it blooms into *versus*—God versus Adam and Eve.

And this is the originating sin—not the thievery of forbidden fruit, but the hostility that occasioned the rebellion. Adam and Eve eat forbidden fruit only because they suspect God is holding out on them, is secretly against them instead of for them. Satan is the original antagonist, the father of hostility, and we are his children. Once upon a time at the beginning of time, we imagined God to be our enemy, and we've been at each other's throats ever since.

PART TWO: EAST OF EDEN

It's no accident the first murder promptly follows humanity's journey east of Eden, and it's not just murder but fratricide—the murder of a brother: "And it came about when they were in the field, that Cain rose up against Abel his brother and killed him" (Gen 4:8).

Old Testament scholar Walter Brueggemann calls this the introduction of the brother problem: "an extended biblical struggle with the reality of the 'brother' as a troubled but crucial part of human destiny."[36] Brothers fight a lot in Genesis, but metaphorically, the brother problem is the norming of hostility, is "us versus them" gathering so much momentum that thousands of years later the brother problem has become the ultimate theological crisis—a crisis not just of life and death, but of salvation and damnation: "We know that we have passed out of death into life, because we love the brethren. He who does not love abides in death. Everyone who hates his brother is a murderer; and you know that no murderer has eternal life abiding in him" (1 John 3:14–15).

We've no clue why God preferred Abel's sacrifice to Cain's, but we know it made Cain angry. And notice how seriously God takes Cain's anger, speaking of it vividly, as an animal lurking, about to pounce: "Sin is crouching at the door; and its desire is for you, but you must master it" (Gen 4:7). Cain doesn't and instead his anger masters him.

I've never understood attempts to explain Cain's motives and thus psychologize the inaugural murder. Why did Cain do it? Because it felt good! You'll be happy to know I've never committed murder and adore my brother, but hate is a hell of a drug, and I've spent much of my life strung out on it. Most of us have. As Zosima, the wise elder in Dostoyevsky's masterpiece, *The Brothers Karamazov*, observes:

> A man who lies to himself is often the first to take offense. *It sometimes feels very good to take offense, doesn't it?* And surely he knows that no one has offended him, and that he himself has invented the offense and told lies just for the beauty of it, that he has exaggerated for the sake of effect, that he has picked on a word and made a mountain out of a pea—he knows all of that, and still he is the first to take offense, he likes feeling offended, it gives him great pleasure, and thus he reaches the point of real hostility . . . because it's not only a pleasure, sometimes it's beautiful to be offended.[37]

And this is your brain on hate—the ecstasy of antagonism, the euphoria of condemnation, the sordid pleasure of self-righteousness. It sometimes feels very good to take offense, doesn't it?

PART THREE: CIVILIZED TO DEATH

Satan gossips hostility into the garden, we imagine God to be our enemy, we imagine each other to be our enemy, and the story of us versus them has sketched the blueprint for an unfriendly world. Construction doesn't take long: "Then Cain went out from the presence of the Lord, and settled in the land of Nod, east of Eden. Cain had relations with his wife and she conceived, and gave birth to Enoch; and Cain built a city . . ." (Gen 4:16–17). Cain commits the first murder then builds the first city. Coincidence?

While strolling through a local bookstore, I did something shamefully shallow and bought a book based on cover and title alone. A sad chimp dressed in a middle-class manager's blazer stares blankly into your eyes. The phone in his hand illuminates his forlorn face and the fast-food burger before him sags under the weight of grease. We've caught him in between swipes and bites; we've caught him in the act of "progress." The title of Christopher Ryan's book? *Civilized to Death: The Price of Progress*. The book is merrily eccentric, making an argument that's just strange enough to be true: everything isn't always getting better.

Nasty, brutish, and short—that's how Thomas Hobbes famously described human life before civilization. Better yet, here's how Rutger Bregman portrays it: "Let's start with a little history lesson: In the past, everything was worse. For roughly 99% of the world's history, 99% of humanity was poor, hungry, dirty, afraid, stupid, sick, and ugly."[38] Excusing Bregman's unforgivable *faux pas* of deriding Neanderthal appearances, that does sound miserable, and we're all familiar with such odes to the triumph of civilization: everything used to be worse, but now everything is getting better! But is it? According to Ryan, no:

> Whether the wonders of our age are worth their exorbitant cost is a question each of us must ultimately ask for ourselves. But before we can begin to answer such a crucial question, we must first cut through the veil of pro-progress propaganda to which we've been subjected for centuries in order to do two things: get a fuller conception of civilization that includes its costs and victims, and think hard about how much meaning and fulfillment "modern wonders" actually bring to our lives. If everything's so amazing, why are so many of us so profoundly unhappy?[39]

From here the book chronicles the ways in which the "progress" of civilization is perhaps better understood as "adaptation"—things are changing, yes, but change doesn't necessarily mean progress. For example, conflict between humans in a pre-civilized world was, by its nature, fairly low-key. When you're a part of a small wandering tribe, your possessions consist of what you feel like carrying around. Without the "luxury" of storage units and trust funds, our uncivilized ancestors quite literally could not accumulate much stuff—only what their arms could hold and legs could bear. And when you have less stuff, there's less stuff to fight over—less to defend, less to take.

In one of the most sobering anecdotes in the book, Ryan notes that while America is the wealthiest nation the world has ever seen, 40 percent of Americans donate less than 2 percent of their income to charity, and 45 percent give nothing at all.[40] He contrasts this with the poor African villager who once told his wife that "the best place for extra food is in my friend's stomach" because when you can't stash your stuff, the decision is clear: it will be shared or it will be spoiled because it cannot be stockpiled.

And Scripture's prescience on this point is both shocking and shockingly under-appreciated. Far from perpetuating the propaganda of progress wherein everything used to be worse but is now getting better, Scripture describes the "civilizing" of humanity as a deeply ambiguous affair. In fact, one could fancy that Genesis 3–11 tells a story in which the fall of humanity results in the rise of civilization—or more provocatively, that the fall of humanity is, in some sense, the rise of civilization.

Is it a fluke that God's plan to redeem fallen creation begins with the call of a wandering Aramean named Abraham instead of a king or pharaoh? Or that the central event of the Old Testament is an exodus from the center of civilization (Egypt) and to the wilderness? I'm not setting out to find Christopher McCandless's abandoned city bus any time soon, but it's enough to make one wonder . . .

In the beginning or shortly thereafter, the story of hostility was introduced to the world, and we've been telling it ever since. This story has been mixed into the mortar of civilization and created people who do not know who they are unless they know who they are against.

According to John Calvin, the human heart is an idol-making factory, constantly churning out new and unworthy objects of worship. This is true, but the human heart is also an enemy-making factory, constantly churning out adversaries and stoking the flames of antagonism. This brings us to the modern chapter in the story of us versus them: hate's search for an acceptable home.

PART FOUR: HATE'S SEARCH FOR AN ACCEPTABLE HOME

Once upon a time, you could hate whoever for whatever. That's slightly hyperbolic, but only slightly. Race, religion, gender, sexuality, nationality, astrology—all were fair game for hostility; hate had many acceptable homes. But we're not allowed to hate like we used to.

Imagine a semi-immortal being called Bob who is fifty thousand years old. In the beginning, Bob is a member of a small family of nomads, and he hates the other family of nomads who, just to spite him, have a habit of urinating on the trees at the perimeter of his territory. Skip forward a few thousand years and now Bob is a member of a larger tribe of farmers, and he hates the neighboring tribe of farmers who occasionally pillage his crops. Skip forward a thousand years and now Bob is a citizen of a nation, and he hates the rival nations jockeying for global conquest. And over these thousands of years, Bob's hate has adapted and always included ethnic, religious, and gender undertones (he's an ancient man, after all), but its infrastructure has been fairly stable: geographically tribal hatred. Bob lives *here*, and he hates people who live *there*.

But then something happens, and Bob's options for hostility not only evolve but narrow in an unprecedented way.

Bob reads Bacon, Descartes, Hume, Kant, Diderot, Locke, Spinoza, and Adam Smith. He even reads a woman named Mary Wollstonecraft who makes the hilarious claim that women should be treated as rational beings! What's next—non-Europeans are people, too? It's a slippery slope. But try as he might to resist, the ideas he imbibes from these thinkers are undeniably persuasive and over time will exert enormous pressure on Bob's moral sensibilities. Eventually, Bob becomes a modern man, and as a modern man he's not allowed to hate people for things they can't control—things like the place of their birth, the color of their skin, or the anatomy of their body. Bob is only allowed to hate people for things they choose—things like religion and politics.

Hate has finally found an acceptable home.

Sixty years ago, interracial marriage was heresy, but now most Americans support it (90 percent or so). Progress! And this progress is real and wonderful, but we must not be duped—remember, everything isn't always getting better, and often change is simply adaptation mimicking progress. Case in point: around 55 percent of Americans now have a problem with "inter-political" marriage![41] We are quite happy to let our son marry a black woman, but letting him marry a Democrat is a bridge too far. After all, we must keep the bloodline pure.

This ostensibly outrageous finding has been documented in study after study, in field after field, yielding the indisputable fact that partisanship now divides us more than race. Ezra Klein summarizes these findings like this:

> The data was everywhere. Polls looking at the difference between how Republicans viewed Democrats and how Democrats viewed Republicans now showed that partisans were less accepting of each other than white people were of black people or than black people were of white people. But there was no way partisanship—an identity we choose and sometimes change—could possibly have become a cleavage in American life as deep as race, right?[42]

Right?

Shanto Iyengar is a big deal, the director of Stanford's Political Communication Laboratory, and he was one of the first to discern enmity's evolution and test it with an ingenious experiment.[43] He gathered one thousand people and had them compare the resumes of two high school seniors competing for a single scholarship. The resumes tinkered with three basic variables: the students' GPA, race, and political affiliation. Sixty years ago, the results of the experiment would have revealed profound racial bias—race would blow academic achievement and political affiliation away as the most determinative factor in who received the scholarship; white people would award the scholarship to the white student, black people would award the scholarship to the black student.

But to Iyengar's surprise, *political affiliation* far outpaced race as the most determinative factor, having far more to do with who received the scholarship than GPA or skin color. You might think Kansas City is in Kansas, but if you were president of the Young Democrats or wore a MAGA hat, that made you scholarship-worthy enough in the eyes of your fellow donkeys or elephants.

But how could this be? Racial animosity runs so deep. Racism is America's original sin. Systemic racism plainly poisons our splendid but sick country. Iyengar's hypothesis evokes hate's aforementioned search for an acceptable home:

> Political identity is fair game for hatred. Racial identity is not. Gender identity is not. You cannot express negative sentiments about social groups in this day and age. But political identities are not protected by these constraints. A Republican is someone who chooses to be a Republican, so I can say whatever I want about them.[44]

I would reckon your life is filled with anecdotes confirming Iyengar's hypothesis—mine is. Like all humans, I harbor racial biases even when I am unaware of them or actively opposing them. While they are powerful instigators of animosity and injustice, I am a modern man, and my battle against them is aided by moral clarity, by the sure and certain knowledge that my racial biases are sinful, and this means they are rigidly policed, by both others and me. To reiterate, this policing does not erase my racial biases, but it does make it more difficult for me to justify them.

But no such policing happens when the topic shifts from race to ideology or politics, and I find justifying my nastiness not only easy but enjoyable.

You can't control your place of birth or skin color, but your decision to be a Democrat is yours and yours alone, and you must be punished for it. You can plead for mercy, but you will find none, because when it comes to ideology, my hatred is not only permissible but righteous—a moral obligation.

Comedian Sarah Silverman suggests hatred's clever ideological costuming is a base expression of "righteousness porn"—modern Western people getting off on shameless self-righteous preening:

> Everyone is throwing the first stone. . . . It's a perversion. . . . It's "Look how righteous I am!" and now I'm gonna press refresh all day long to see how many likes I get on my righteousness. . . . There's so much to be genuinely outraged by, but you have to ask yourself whether the action you're taking is creating change or creating further division.[45]

But is a little righteousness porn so wrong? We've clearly rationalized and justified our ideological hatred, but perhaps for good reason. Perhaps ideology is an acceptable home for hate. It all comes down to who narrates the master script for the world as you know it.

CHRISTIANITY'S ANNOYING BURDEN

Christians shoulder the annoying burden of being unable to justify their hatred.

Other religions and non-religions must grapple with the morality of hatred on their own terms, based on their own stories and the values embedded therein, but to be a Christian is to submit to the story set forth in Scripture, culminating in Christ and passed down through the ages. This story claims God's joyful justice is the end to which all creation is drawn. Furthermore, this story claims no injustice will be glossed, but no hatred will be permitted. Injustice will be given no quarter, but hatred is not and cannot be a means to God's joyfully just future.

Why? Because the ends are the means in the process of becoming.[46] This is a fancy way to say the destination is shaped by the journey, and we cannot arrive at God's kingdom by pathways of hostility. God himself certainly didn't! Indeed, the central act of Christian faith is God consuming our hostility with searing love, not to tolerate injustice and sin, but rather to smother it under the weight of divine glory.

> For while we were still helpless, at the right time Christ died for the ungodly.... God demonstrates His own love toward us in that while we were yet sinners, Christ died for us.... For if while we were enemies we were reconciled to God through the death of His Son, much more, having been reconciled, we shall be saved by His life. (Rom 5:6, 8, 10)

This doesn't mean we've been assigned a life of indifference or peppy optimism. Jesus himself was no moderate man, but an extremist who blistered his opponents with rhetoric so hot it still radiates off the red letters. Meek and mild Jesus was not, and milquetoast moderation is not a beatitude. But neither is hatred. In a letter to the church at Ephesus, the apostle Paul counsels we navigate our hostility like this: "Be angry, and yet don't sin; do not let the sun go down on your anger" (Eph 4:26).

Be angry! Don't gloss injustice. Don't tolerate exploitation. Brook no compromise with sin. That's a command! And yet in your anger, don't sin. How? Don't let the sun go down on your anger. When has the sun gone down on your anger? When you let it spend the night... and then another, and another. The sun has gone down on your anger when anger has made your heart its home and given hatred squatter's rights, and that is sin.

In fairness, there's nothing more natural than treating an enemy like an enemy, just as there's nothing more defensible in the modern world than ideological hatred. But we don't have the right to tell Christianity's story however we see fit, and the one who does have the rights on our story has forbidden unloved enemies. I do not know if this is *humanly* possible, though I suspect it's not; I only know it's the story Christianity tells, and it tells no other.

Righteous anger? Yes—it's not only permissible, but commanded. Noble hatred? No—not even a liberal (or conservative). And if the unspoken and de facto litmus test for whether anger is righteous or unrighteous is whether it's yours or theirs (and surely it is for most of us), some further questions are begging to be asked.

But we do rather enjoy having enemies and feel lost without them. One such name given to this antagonism addiction is "St. George in Retirement Syndrome."[47] Once a brave warrior slayed an evil dragon. It was glorious. For the rest of his days he sought out other dragons, needing the fight and the glory. So he slayed the big dragons, then the medium dragons, then the smaller dragons, until there were no more dragons. But he still needed the dragons; he did not know who he was without them. So he ended his days slaying the thin air, imagining it to contain dragons. Many of us share St. George's malady and have identities that are unstable because they are overly determined by antagonisms. This is the problem with needing an enemy.

Reflecting on lessons learned over the course of his time developing black theology, James Cone stated his regret that black theology was formed too much in reaction to white racism. While understandable and perhaps inevitable, this was problematic because it implied black theology needed white racism, and Cone believed black theology's future would largely depend on its ability to wean itself off dependence on white racism and account for itself on more constructive grounds. Cone believed black theology's beauty and power did not and could not depend indefinitely on the foil of white racism. Cone believed "one's theological vision must be derived from something more than merely a reaction to one's enemy."[48] Surely Cone is channeling Christ, for while having enemies is inevitable, and perhaps even mandatory this side of the kingdom, we dare not need them. If your faith needs enemies, you need a better faith.

A brief history of a long history of hate shows hostility has been on a long migration over the ages, seeking safe havens and respectable forms. The father of hostility is alive and well, and the human heart is an enemy-making factory. We've hated each other because of tribe, nationality, geography, gender, race, religion, ideology, and if we ever discover aliens, I'm certain we will find a way to hate them too. This is systemic hostility, antagonism's anthem, us versus them. It's one of the most powerful stories creating the world, and most of us don't know how to be *us* without a *them*.

But Christianity tells a better story—a story where the most important thing about *you* is not *them*, a story where our identity is rooted in the God who is for us and not the people who are against us.

3

The Coddling of the American Church
How the Big Sort Creates Communities of Spite, Sameness, and Sedentary Faith

> Jesus summoned his twelve disciples and gave them authority over unclean spirits, to cast them out, and to heal every kind of disease and every kind of sickness. Now the names of the twelve apostles are these: The first, Simon, who is called Peter, and Andrew his brother; and James the son of Zebedee, and John his brother; Philip and Bartholomew; Thomas and Matthew the tax collector; James the son of Alphaeus, and Thaddaeus; Simon the Zealot, and Judas Iscariot, the one who betrayed Him. (Matt 10:1–4)

ONE IMAGINES ANDREW, THE brother of Simon Peter, is thrilled to hear his name called second. Perhaps he is riding his brother's coattails into such a pole position, a possibility he cheerfully overlooks because when all is said and done, who cares? Now a founding member of Jesus' cabinet, he listens with approval as Jesus summons James, John, Philip, Bartholomew, and Thomas—all sane and sensible selections. But then Jesus begins to bungle his draft.

Matthew the tax collector?

Andrew assumes he must have heard wrongly, but then infamous Matthew hesitantly emerges from the crowd, looking every bit as stunned as Andrew. It was odd enough Jesus had previously invited Matthew to tag along (Matt 9:9), but a further invitation into the inner circle was ridiculous because, not to put too fine a point on it, Matthew was a damned thief!

He collected Roman taxes from his own people and then lined his own pockets by over-taxing his own people. Save maybe his mother, nobody liked Matthew, but Andrew found him particularly vile. Andrew, after all, had previously been a disciple of John the Baptist, and John was not the most tolerant bloke—a wild man who lived in the wild, ate bugs, and verbally harassed visitors. It's been speculated that John the Baptist was associated with the Essenes, a Jewish group known for fastidious sectarianism; Essenes felt faithfulness to Yahweh was best embodied by a rigid holiness that required a certain separation from the world. Andrew knew Jesus ran a looser ship than John, but his inner Essene is throwing a fit as the tax collector stands beside him.

Jesus next calls James the son of Alphaeus, and Andrew nods, worried about keeping the Jameses straight but happy to see order restored with another solid choice. Every group needs a charity case, and maybe that was Matthew's role. Makes sense, but what happens next does not.

Simon the Zealot?

Andrew lets out an involuntary gasp because while Matthew the tax collector was a damned thief, Simon the Zealot was a damned maniac—an extremist freedom fighter with no qualms about spilling blood in the name of Jewish liberation and Roman eradication. Matthew is vile, but Simon is vicious. Andrew is so stunned that the final selection of the squirrely Judas Iscariot barely registers. Andrew looks around the inner circle he imagined would be a band of brothers, and he instead sees a posse of opposites and enemies.

Andrew the Essene thinks withdrawal from Rome is the answer; Matthew the tax collector thinks compromise with Rome is the answer; Simon the Zealot thinks war with Rome is the answer. One wonders if Israel contained three men who disagreed about more.[49] What is Jesus doing?

Jesus summons twelve men as a sign he's fulfilling God's promise to the twelve tribes of Israel, as a sign his work is God's covenant faithfulness to Israel in action. Jesus and his chosen family are Abraham's sons, blessed by God in order to bless all the families of the earth in the name of Abraham's God. But why does the chosen family include such contradiction and incongruity? Why an even number of such oddly fitting people?

Because Cain rose up and killed Abel and Abel's blood still cries out— not for retribution that's been delayed, but for communion that's been lost.

Abel's blood cries out because Abel lost his brother, and he needs God to return him. Jesus summons a mismatched, clashing family of Cains and Abels as a sign he's undoing the eighth day—giving Adam back to Eve and Eve back to Adam, giving creation back to humans and humans back to creation. Jesus is giving Abel his brother back.

Jesus summons this odd family, not *despite* their differences, but *because* of them. Jesus summons this odd family because his gospel is the good news of the redemption and reunion of humanity—a convergence that is not the crushing, monolithic singularity of a black hole, but the raucous gathering of a cosmic family reunion. Peter Leithart has said this well: "Divided humanity is reunited as the family of the heavenly Father, in the body of the Son, as the temple of the Spirit. . . . The church is reunited humanity, the social manifestation of the gospel of Jesus. The church is salvation itself in social form."[50]

I'm not too proud to admit this takes my breath away: the church is the reunion of humanity, salvation itself in social form, the future made present, the fullness of the Christ who is the fullness of everything![51] Only a cold heart could fail to be warmed by such a radiant vision, but it's a vision rarely glimpsed because, as Lohfink stated earlier, the church has often been the stumbling block instead of the threshold, the shattered mirror that makes possible the world's unbelief instead of the icon that portends its eschatological reunion.

THE INCREASINGLY INCURIOUS CASE OF ARTHUR MILLER

"How can the polls be neck and neck when I don't know one Bush supporter?"[52]

Arthur Miller spoke for many Democrats in the lead-up to the 2000 presidential election. All the yards in his neighborhood were undoubtedly decorated with signs supporting Al Gore, and George W. Bush was the oft-bludgeoned piñata in jokes among friends. The world was blue, and he knew it, so how were polls predicting a close election? More difficult to spot in the wild than Sasquatch, where the hell were these elusive Bush supporters? Increasingly, we are all poor, befuddled Arthur Miller: surrounded by sameness and perpetually surprised to learn the world as we know it is not the world.

In the 1976 presidential election, only 26 percent of Americans lived in landslide counties (counties where one party won by twenty percentage points or more). This means most Americans lived in politically and ideologically diverse counties, counties with lots of Republicans, lots of Democrats, and thus few Arthur Millers. But since then American counties have been growing less ideologically diverse and more segregated, meaning sightings of ideological opposites have become rarer and rarer, and in the 2016 election over 60 percent of Americans now lived in landslide counties.[53] This phenomenon was first documented and named by Bill Bishop, who wrote a book about it called *The Big Sort: Why the Clustering of Like-Minded America is Tearing Us Apart.*

The basic premise of "The Big Sort" is simple and indisputable: American society is experiencing an unprecedented and accelerating sorting in which like-minded people are clustering together geographically. A mere fifty years ago, most Americans were, quite literally, surrounded by lots of people who thought differently; now, most are surrounded by an entourage of ideological groupies. But how did this happen? Where did Arthur Miller come from?

Suppose you could spend a day with a dear friend who agrees with you on most matters of consequence or a stranger who disagrees with you on most matters of consequence. Unless you're a social sadist, you would tend to choose a day spent with an agreeable friend over a day with a disagreeable stranger. Why? Well it's not because you're a crotchety, misanthropic prude; it's because one experience is pleasant and the other likely unpleasant. It's because given the choice, we usually choose sameness.

And this scenario, playing itself out millions (billions? trillions?) of times a day over years and years has amplified itself into The Big Sort. Over the last fifty years, technology has created choices that did not previously exist, which has created a mobility that did not previously exist, which has transformed modern life from à la carte to buffet. Unless they loaded their entire life into a wagon and braved a brush with death by dysentery on the Oregon Trail, my great, great, great grandparents were stuck living where they were born. Many if not most of us could relocate anywhere in the country in a few days.

One particularly ironic wrinkle is that whereas a lack of mobility enforced racial and cultural segregation in early America, hypermobility encourages ideological separation in modern America. When we can choose who we'll surround ourselves with, we tend to surround ourselves with sameness, though we are mostly unaware we're doing it.

Donald Green, a political scientist at Yale, invites us to imagine walking into a building where two parties are happening. In the room to the left, there's a cocktail party filled with liberals and progressives; to the right, a tailgate filled with conservatives. How would you decide which party to attend? Rather than meticulously mapping out a decision tree, you'd look at both parties and sense a vibe, and you'd be drawn to the party with people whose sons and daughters you'd like your sons and daughters to marry. How would you decide which party to attend? Easy: the party that's filled with your kind of people.[54]

Case in point, I bought my first house in a fairly diverse neighborhood near a college campus. Given the economic restraints of a first-time homeowner whose savings account balance included no commas, my options were limited. Years passed, the commas came, the buffet opened, and I purchased my second house in a newer neighborhood with larger lots, more trees, and, as it turned out, lots of people who acted, thought, looked, and lived suspiciously like I did. How did this happen? While I certainly didn't intend to end up in Stepford, I was given a choice to choose, and I was instinctively drawn to a place filled with people who felt like my kind of people.

As a brief aside, it's often asserted the fundamental difference in conservatives and progressives is a trait difference, typically reducible to biologically determined dispositions, which cause some people to be averse to novelty (conservatives) and others to be drawn to it (progressives).[55] From here we inevitably get a heavy-handed annotation about progressives desiring diversity while conservatives are scared of it—"Sorting has made Democrats more diverse and Republicans more homogenous . . . has made the Democrats into a coalition of difference and driven Republicans further into sameness."[56] There is something true here, but the truth is far from categorical *because when it comes to ideology*, conservatives and progressives are equally fond of inbreeding—a fact delightfully illustrated by an episode of *Curb Your Enthusiasm*.

Larry David is the show's creator, writer, and protagonist—a nominally liberal Jewish fellow living in LA, surrounded by fellow WASP-allergic liberals. Larry is also a curmudgeon, and so after having his arm twisted into having lunch with someone he rather dislikes, he's scheming for a way out when a friend casually mentions the disdain he has for Trump supporters: "I'd never play golf with a Trump supporter. Walking around town with those Make America Great Again hats. I don't need that crap." The lightbulbs go off for Larry, and the next day he shows up for his dreaded lunch date wearing (you guessed it) a MAGA hat. Larry's lunch date is so horrified at the prospect of being seen in public with Larry and his red lid that he immediately contrives an excuse to leave, and Larry spends the rest of the episode brazenly sauntering around LA in his MAGA hat as liberals flee in terror and long lines part before him like the Red Sea.

Summarizing the geographically ideological sorting of modern America, Bruce Oppenheimer suggests it's ultimately reducible to "the increased mobility of Americans and the corresponding growth in the freedom to select where they will reside."[57] Given the choice, we tend to choose sameness.

Predictably, the ideological sorting of actual neighborhoods is concurrently occurring in digital neighborhoods.

THE INCREASINGLY INCURIOUS CASE OF ARTHUR MILLER 2.0

"Odd, angry cul-de-sacs."[58]

Ezra Klein employs this phrase while commenting on the state of affairs created by modern media, and it's as fitting a description as one can find for the balkanized digital world. Far more malleable than the world of brick and mortar, the digital world is a voluntarist's dream—maximum customization, minimal prescription. And as the civil engineers of our respective digital worlds, we've constructed uncivil and segregated digital neighborhoods orbiting odd, angry cul-de-sacs. Given the godlike opportunity to fashion the digital world how we see fit, we inevitably create it in our own sequestered image.

In *Homo Deus*—a book both naively bombastic and soberly lucid—Yuval Noah Harari explores possible futures for humanity, offering probabilities rather than prophecies, and one of the things he finds probable is a future in which humans increasingly cede control of our lives to algorithms. By nature a skeptic, I've always laughed off fears of judgement day by Skynet, and I still do. The robots aren't coming for us. But what Harari describes is far more chilling than a robotic doomsday because it seems benevolent:

> The shifting of authority from humans to algorithms is happening all around us, not as a result of some momentous governmental decision, but due to a flood of mundane personal choices.[59]

> This is not an apocalyptic scenario. Algorithms won't revolt and enslave us. Rather, they will be so good at making decisions for us that it would be madness not to follow their advice.[60]

The robots aren't coming to annihilate; the algorithms are coming to help! Chances are you already trust algorithms to invest your money, inform your medical decisions, prepare your entertainment options, and curate your news feed. Modern people have far too many choices to make to make many of them well, and the algorithms help shoulder our cognitive load. Hooray, algorithms!

But when we peer into the shadows cast by our shining algorithms, we glimpse many disconcerting developments because while the algorithmic brick and mortar of the digital world is, in a sense, amoral, we are not. And in the digital neighborhoods we construct for ourselves via media and social media, the algorithms are simply much too good at giving us what we want: outrage, self-righteousness, and tribal preening.

In screeds railing against partisanship, blanket condemnations of modern media and technology are common—there's a conspiracy to divide us! But there's no conspiracy. We designed the algorithms to give us what we want, and, as it turns out, we want puppy or kitten videos (puppy if you're conservative; kitten if you're liberal)[61] and a healthy portion of spite. If it infuriates, it leads—this organizing principle of modern media is baked into all the algorithms because in an increasingly scarce attention economy, our attention must be grabbed, and nothing grabs our attention like a fight. Jia Tolentino says it all quite well:

> The early internet had been constructed around lines of affinity and openness. But when the internet moved to an organizing principle of opposition, much of what had formerly been surprising and rewarding and curious became tedious, noxious, and grim.... It's much easier to organize people against something than it is to unite them in an affirmative vision. And, within the economy of attention, conflict always gets more people to look.[62]

It should not shock us to hear spite-based diets are bad for us. Specifically, the spite-based diets made increasingly tempting and convenient by modern media make us, in a word, dumber. A 2018 study measured people's capacity to accurately understand ideological others, and the results were as hilarious as they were depressing. Democrats, for example, believed 44 percent of Republicans earned over $250,000 a year—Democrats believed almost half of Republicans were rich, privileged, economic libertarians, swimming around in a vault of gold bars while complaining about paying taxes.

Two percent of Republicans make over $250,000 a year.

Republicans, meanwhile, believed 38 percent of Democrats were gay, lesbian, or bisexual—Republicans believed over of third of Democrats were non-hetero Ls, Gs, Bs, Ts, Qs, and +s.

Six percent of Democrats are gay, lesbian, or bisexual.[63]

These findings are comical and sobering, but the truly disturbing discovery was that this profound misperception of ideological others was greatest among those who were *most* politically interested and informed—the more political media you consumed, the dumber you became about "others."[64] Spite makes you stupid.

And while there are some ideological climate change deniers out there, this inconvenient truth is increasingly acknowledged, and attempts have been made to reckon with it, but thus far all attempts have been ineffective or downright counterproductive. Take attempts to tweak the algorithms so we encounter the thoughts and posts of people who disagree with us—say, an algorithm designed to drop the occasional post from a conservative into the feed of a liberal. Surely that will help! As it turns out, it not only does not help, but it hurts. Exposure to ideological others on social media mostly creates rebuttal and further radicalization, not reflection, which is not surprising result given most modern media is aimed at preening and not persuasion.[65]

We create the algorithms, the algorithms create us, we and the algorithms create more *us versus them*. Our actual neighborhoods are sorted, our digital neighborhoods are sorted, and, in what constitutes nothing less than a betrayal of the gospel, our churches are increasingly sorted too.[66]

BLUE PEOPLE, RED PEOPLE, PURPLE WINE

During the COVID-19 pandemic and resulting quarantine measures, my church enlisted the help of local health authorities to create a process that would allow us to gather responsibly for worship. This process involved strict social distancing guidelines, strict capacity guidelines, and mandating masks. And initially, most people gladly complied because everyone was thrilled to be able to gather at all, but that mood soured abruptly as wearing or not wearing a mask morphed into yet another boring opportunity to divide ourselves into us and them—refusing to wear a mask on your face marked your allegiance every bit as clearly as a Trump sign staked in your lawn. And then people started leaving.

I think it's safe to say that in my decade at my church, our largest single exodus of people occurred, not because of a theological shift or staffing overhaul or pastoral malfeasance, but because people refused to wear a mask for an hour a week amid a global pandemic. And perhaps they would have left no matter what, but their leaving was made considerably easier because a nearby church was not mandating masks during worship, a church considerably more conservative than ours in most ways (except, ironically, on masks). Their leaving was made easy because they had options.

I've often wondered how this ripple—my church losing many of our conservative members and an already conservative church gaining even more conservative members, and certainly vice versa—will surge across the space and time of our community. I think of the lost communion table where blue and red people will no longer share purple wine. I think of the ideologically diverse friendships between my children and theirs that could have been but now will not be. I think of the church my grandchildren will inherit, which will inevitably be a church more sorted than the one I knew and pastored because it seems unlikely the sorting stops.

Most of the New Testament could probably be categorized as a theology of conflict resolution. The gospel is the good news of God's commitment to resolve conflict, in all its vertical and horizontal vectors, on God's own terms, first and foremost in the church. But modern, sorted people like us cannot help but find all this biblical teaching on conflict resolution both baffling and irrelevant because we don't need to resolve our conflicts.

We don't need guidance on handling contentious disagreements, or administering and submitting to discipline, or reconciling people deeply at odds. We don't need conflict resolution; we need directions to the church a few streets over that better suits our preferences; we need the podcast link to the preacher who will pet our ideology. We don't need to resolve our conflicts because we have the luxury of simply walking away from them. After all, why resolve when you can just leave? But this luxury is also our curse.

Imagine you're a Christian in ancient Corinth. We know from Paul the church there was madly mercurial: rife with petty vendettas, special interest groups, pseudo-enlightened factions, and one man proudly bedding his stepmother. And suppose you're a prudential Puritan at heart—you're disgusted by the moral laxity, and you long for a purer church. So you schedule a meeting with the leaders of your church and make your case: we've got to drain the swamp, purge ourselves of all deplorables, kick out everybody who doesn't meet the (= my) standard of holiness. And the leaders hear you out and agree the gent fornicating with his stepmom has crossed the moral Rubicon, but they disagree with your ultimate proposal. They're not going to kick out everybody who doesn't meet your standard of holiness.

And you're furious! How dare they! Can't they see? Many things run through your mind as you stomp back home, but one thing does not: it never even occurs to you to leave your church. Because you're angry enough to leave, but where would you go? There's one church in town. Are you righteous enough to march your stubborn bum fifty miles on foot every Sunday to attend the church in Athens that practices strict kosher laws and is walking verse by verse through Leviticus for the next five years? No. You will not leave, and you will not even think of leaving because leaving is a luxury you do not have. You are cursed, you are blessed, with staying.

THE CODDLING OF THE AMERICAN CHURCH

There are good reasons to leave a church, but the bar for leaving is set in direct proportion to the number of alternative options, meaning more options inevitably sets a lower bar for leaving, and modern American Christians have *many* (too many?) options. I once saw a promotional video for a new church plant in which the planter explained he'd chosen this location because there were so few churches. The video concludes with a drone shot from high above surveying the locale, a shot in which *five* other churches are immediately visible.

There are good reasons to leave a church, and a certain degree of choice can be a good thing, but the available buffet necessitates that modern American Christians don't have to make it work in the way ancient Christians did. To be more accurate, we don't have to make it work in the way most Christians throughout the world still do. To be more accurate yet, we don't have to make it work in the way most every Christian in the history of the world has had to make it work. Most every Christian in the history of the world has been blessed with the curse of having to make it work, cursed with the blessing of staying.

With certain exceptions, leaving is the curse that feels like a blessing whereas staying is the blessing that can feel like a curse. This is hard to perceive and nearly impossible to feel in the moment. Some marriages need to end, but most do not, and I long ago lost count of the number of people who divorced one sinner only to marry another and inherit a new set of marital struggles equal to or surpassing those they fled.

Commenting on the farcical modern fantasy of limitlessness (specifically in relation to humans and natural resources), Wendell Berry argues that humans and the natural world not only plainly have limits, but that a proper embrace of limits leads to a kind of inexhaustibility that far surpasses what "limitlessness" can achieve. If you treat an acre of land as if it has no limits, as if it can be pushed, used, and abused at your whim, then you will ruin the land. Treat the acre as if it's "limitless," and you'll ensure it is not.

But if you respect the limits of the acre by seeking to make the most of it within the boundaries of what it can and can't bear, then there is a sense in which that acre can become an inexhaustible source of life, bearing healthy soil, trees, and crops indefinitely. Inexhaustibility springs, not from limitlessness, but from limits. Broadening the point, Berry quotes a wise teacher's observation that people will "never be worth a damn as long as they've got two choices."[67] We will never make the most of anything so long as we can always choose another thing.

One of the direct and dire consequences of our ecclesial promiscuity is we have an ever-diminishing capacity for dealing with conflict in a healthy manner because conflict resolution is a muscle built up through usage—if you don't use it, you lose it, which means chronic leaving leads to atrophy. It makes us happy now but fragile over time. If you've ever wondered why your nerves are frayed, your patience is thin, your aptitude for constructive disagreement is inept, and your mental health deteriorates in dog years yet you're only twenty and have lived a comfortable life, it's likely largely due to the fragility that is the fruit of conflict resolution atrophy. If mocking conservatives on Facebook is you marching from Selma, or trolling progressives on Twitter/X is you storming the beaches of Normandy, chances are your conflict muscles could use some toning.

There is a sentiment, variously attributed to St. Augustine, John Chrysostom, and countless others, that the church should be conceived as a "hospital for sinners, not a museum for saints." Jesus says something rather like this: "It is not those who are well who need a physician, but those who are sick. I have not come to call the righteous but sinners to repentance."[68] It's a beautiful and biblical metaphor, but it's a metaphor that needs to be supplemented lest it become kitsch sentimentality, and who better to put the kibosh on sentimentality than John Calvin?

In an oft-neglected emphasis of his work, Calvin envisioned the church as a gym of sorts—a place we work out our intellectual, moral, aesthetic, and spiritual muscles.[69] Church is not a drive-through where we gorge ourselves on spite and sameness while settling into a sedentary faith. Church is a ring where we spar *biblically*, where we submit, over the long haul, to practices that make our faith as tough as it is gentle, as resilient as it is kind. The church is a hospital where sinners find healing, yes (!), but it's also a gym where sinners galvanize grit. And had you indeed been a Christian living in ancient Corinth, St. Paul would have reminded you and your bickering church of this very thing: "Therefore I run in such a way, as not without aim; I box in such a way, as not beating the air; but I discipline my body and make it my slave, so that, after I have preached to others, I myself will not be disqualified."[70]

Jonathan Haidt and Greg Lukianoff wrote a sensational book titled *The Coddling of the American Mind: How Good Intentions and Bad Ideas are Setting Up a Generation for Failure*. Among other things, the book examines modern American culture's cult of "safety-ism," a cultural mood in which we are quick to coddle and shelter in place because we're worried that we and our children can't handle the big, bad world. And while we should take proper precautions, safety-ism is deeply flawed because the world can never be made *safe* or even safe *enough* once safety becomes an obsession. So rather than making the world as safe as possible, we must aim at making ourselves and our children *resilient*. Somewhat paradoxically, if you aim at safety what you tend to get instead is fragility, and once fragility sets in, the world can never be safe enough.

It seems the American church has gone the way of the American mind and is currently reaping the fruits of fragility commensurate with a long season of outlandish coddling. Given the choice to choose, we choose to sort by sameness, and this sorting makes us spiteful, stolid, and fragile. Were Jesus to summon a modern American Andrew, Matthew, and Simon together, they would surely part ways, start competing podcasts, and plant three separate churches as soon as Jesus turned his back.

It's a drab and dreary set of affairs, but, for Christians, the good news is always better than the bad news, and the good news is that the church's call is also its sure and certain destiny. When all is said and done, we will be what God says we are: the redemption and reunion of humanity. To that end, we reverberate the future by practicing it in the present because that *is* faith. How?

Practicing God's future includes a great many practices but is rendered possible or impossible because of one thing: our willingness or unwillingness to stop sorting, stay put, spar, and beat our antagonistic swords into plowshares. God's future becomes present in the form of actual, local, non-metaphorical churches where the gospel is unsorting us into the odd and joyful family we will one day be.

4

The Day of Small Things
Learning to Think Little

IN ORDER TO SAVE America, a mob of people stormed the United States Capitol on January 6, 2021. It was mostly men, and their cause was sure: the recent presidential election, like the country, had been stolen from them, and they would take it back. Were it not for the loss of life, the episode might be remembered with a certain incredulous amusement—this angry mob of men believed they were called and capable of saving a country!

As I watched the footage of them storming, yelling, fighting, destroying, and "saving" their country, I wondered how many of these America-saving insurrectionists had not spoken to their father in decades; I wondered how many had a spouse who despised them; I wondered how many had children who had not felt a father's embrace in years. These angry men imagined themselves responsible for saving America, but could they responsibly tend a single household?

At the end of his letter to the churches of Galatia, the apostle Paul embarrasses us: "So then, while we have opportunity, let us do good to all people, and especially to those who are of the household of the faith" (Gal 6:10). The sentence starts out promising: let us do good to all people! This is the counsel of a visionary, modern man. We are, after all, global citizens of a global community, so our charity can know no bounds. But then the global vision narrows into something archaically parochial: *especially to those who are of the household of the faith.*

While asserting our obligations to "all people," Paul then additionally asserts that our obligations to the Christian household, in some way, supersede our obligations to "all people." Why? Because despite its inclusive veneer Christianity is just another bigoted sect? A tempting accusation at times, but we should give Paul more credit considering, apart from Jesus himself, perhaps no one did more to "globalize" humanity than the man formally known as Saul of Tarsus. And so why does Paul say we should *especially* do good to those who are of the household of the faith?

Have you ever tried to do good to everybody? I did—once. It did not go well. Everybody is a lot of people, and neither I nor I plus the Spirit in me has it in me to do that much good. In the altruistic arithmetic animating the universe, the principle seems to be that attempting to do good to everybody leads to little good done for anybody. As it is with an acre of land, so it is with a human life: limitlessness begets exhaustion; proper limits beget inexhaustibility. Paul understands this, and since he is a planter and tender of actual churches first and a philosophizer second, he wants to guarantee these Galatian churches are inexhaustible. So he tells them to be hardy instead of weary—"don't lose heart in doing good; we'll reap if we don't grow weary" (Gal 6:9)—and then explains how: do good to all, *especially* those of the household of faith.

In the best explanation one is likely to find for what the church is, Gerhard Lohfink says this:

> It can only be that God begins in a small way, at one single place in the world. There must be a place, visible, tangible, where the salvation of the world can begin: that is, where the world becomes what it is supposed to be according to God's plan. Beginning at that place, the new thing can spread abroad. . . . Everyone must have the opportunity to come and see. . . . What drives them to the new thing cannot be force, not even moral pressure, but only the fascination of a world that is changed.[71]

So if we are to be what we are—God's future made imperfectly present in the form of actual, non-metaphorical locales of faithfulness to Jesus (= churches)—then we must prioritize practicing it where we actually are. We must be visible places in the world where God's salvation begins. Hauerwas seconds this motion: "Rather than engage in such grand projects, the church's main task is to be what we are—God's salvation."[72]

This is not to exclude those who are not where we are but to make plain our situation: we will either do good to those (literally) around us or we will do little lasting good to anyone because we are not good at doing good to those we are not with. Do good, especially to the household of faith (*your* household of faith), not to give outsiders the cold shoulder, but so churches radiate the joyful justice that beckons a chilled world with its warmth.

SOFTWARE SOLUTIONS, HARDWARE PROBLEMS

For most of history, most humans knew very few people. From time immemorial, our ancestors knew their tribe, knew of neighboring tribes, and knew nobody besides. From time immemorial, most humans only knew and *knew of* a few hundred people, maybe less. The marks of this smaller social world are sculpted into the architecture of the human brain, which is to say sculpted into the architecture of humanity. Formed in the providential processes of deep time, the human brain is structured to thrive in smaller social environments. Although we can reckon lineage in different ways, clearly vast ages of life in small-scale communities have carved pathways in our brains and landscapes in our humanity that cannot be negated or filled in, no more than ancient glacial gorges can be instantaneously erased from the physical landscape because they're deemed inconvenient.

Reality always wins, and reality stipulates that humans are made to live small, not large; to think little, not big.

"One death is a tragedy; a million is a statistic." Joseph Stalin supposedly said this, and we all know it is true. We cannot compute tragedy beyond a rather small scale because we cannot compute humanity beyond a rather small scale. Beyond the bounds of our basic social capacity, people necessarily become abstractions instead of persons. Reflecting on the transition from pre-civilized humanity to civilization, Christopher Ryan observes that "once human communities grew beyond the point where every individual had a direct relationship with everyone else, something fascinating and terrible happened: Other people became abstractions."[73]

Similarly, Joseph Heath spells out the interface problem encountered when humanity's modest relational hardware merges with modernity's globalized world:

> When it comes to large-scale cooperation, we humans have clearly exceeded our programming. We have become what biologists call an ultrasocial species, despite having a set of social instincts that are essentially tailored for managing life in small-scale tribal

society. It's crucial to recognize, however, that we have not accomplished this by reprogramming ourselves or overcoming our innate design limitations.[74]

Humanity has become an ultrasocial species, living in gargantuan relational networks, managing more interactions in a day than our ancestors might have managed in a hundred lifetimes. But the scope of the change is lost on most of us because it has happened so quickly. Most of us cannot remember a time when hundreds or thousands of strangers were unable to intrude on our lives at any given moment through social media. So we have rapidly become an ultrasocial species, but our neural biology and resulting social instincts have not evolved past their primal tribal formation, which means we are negotiating a relational load we are not designed to bear.

Stanley Milgram is the social psychologist who coined the notion of "six degrees of separation" and also did groundbreaking work on the psychological harshness of life in big cities, using the term "overload" to describe the phenomenon in which people living in big cities are bombarded with so many stimuli (sights, sounds, people) that they're prone to greater stress, anxiety, fear, and at greater risk of "blowing a fuse."[75] Similarly, evolutionary psychologist Robin Dunbar famously posited 150 people as the outer limit of a human's social network—beyond this "we simply do not have the computational capacity to manage social relationships effectively."[76]

So if you've ever felt you don't know the people closest to you as well as you should, yet feel chronically guilty you haven't spent more time getting to know your many acquaintances better, yet also fear there are infinite others you should know or know of but don't, then you have felt the colossal cross-pressure of the modern relational dilemma. You know and know of and are beating yourself up for not knowing too many damn people!

From here, one can draw a fairly straight line to the "epidemic of loneliness" that US Surgeon General Vivek Murthy declared a blight on modern life in 2017—a declaration confirmed by a number of sobering statistics, such as the astonishing fact that over 25 percent of American households are now one-person households (up from 0 percent for basically all of human history), or that when asked how many close confidants they have, the most common answer among Americans is now *zero*.[77] Facing overload, we combust or shut down.

And most importantly, *this is not a software problem*. There is and will be no update to fix it. Try the yoga, the therapy, the mindfulness, the latest calendar app, but those are software solutions to hardware problems.

Reality always wins, and reality stipulates that you are not and will never be a citizen of "the world." Reality stipulates we do not know how to know this many people well, which returns us to the quote from Joseph Heath.

Having stated that our small-scale tribal instincts are not well suited to our new ultrasocial environment, Heath suggests we have coped by "tricking ourselves into feeling as though we are still living in small-scale tribal societies, even when we are not."[78] In other words, we now live in a global world, but we fool ourselves into feeling as though we still live in small tribes, and this delusion helps pacify our smaller social instincts. And while Heath has astutely diagnosed humanity's social hardware problem and inadequate software solutions, his (mis)contention that we are now global creatures pretending to be local creatures only reveals how difficult it is to plumb the depths of the con.

No! We are not ultrasocial, global creatures pretending we are still local, but we are what we have always been, which is precisely the opposite: we are and will always be local, parish creatures who live small or don't live at all, but we have deluded ourselves into believing we are becoming global citizens of a global community. The con is not that we pretend to live small while we actually live big; the con is imagining we could ever do anything other than live small. Imagine yourself to be whatever you like, but you will never do anything other than inhabit one square foot of earth at a time. And as Gottfried von Herder poignantly (if also a bit condescendingly) observed many years ago, "The savage who loves himself, his wife, and child with quiet joy and glows with [the] limited activity of his tribe as for his own life is in my opinion a more real being than that cultivated shadow who is enraptured with the shadow of the whole species."[79]

Planetary.

This is the adjective of choice for the environmental movement, and it's an ambitious word. In preserving the environment, we face a *planetary* problem. But with withering candor, Wendell Berry exposes Oz and reminds us why it's silly to call something, even the environmental crisis, a planetary problem:

> The word *planetary* refers to an abstract anxiety . . . that is desperate and useless exactly to the extent that it is abstract. How, after all, can anybody do anything to heal a planet. The suggestion that anybody could do so is preposterous. The heroes of abstraction keep galloping in on their white horses to save the planet—and they keep falling off in front of the grandstand. . . . The adjective *planetary* describes a problem in such a way that it cannot

> be solved. In fact, though we now have serious problems nearly everywhere on the planet, we have no problem that can accurately be described as planetary.... There are also no national, state, or county problems, and no national, state, or county solutions....
> The problems, if we describe them accurately, are all ... small.[80]

We modern humans face many problems, chief among them our tendency to frame problems in planetary dimensions that ensure nothing can be done but that much dread, anxiety, and rage will surely be felt. Berry offers the smelling salt that might snap us out of our stupor: look closely enough and the problems, all of them, are not planetary, but small. And his prescription—for the healing of our planet in particular, and the healing of a great many other things by implication—is that we must learn how to reduce our problems to the scale of our competence.[81]

How do we know all this to be true? Because every sensible solution offered by every sane and sapient person to any of modern humanity's many big problems is a variation on the smallest of themes: love your neighbor.

OBAMA, JENNINGS, KLEIN, DOSTOYEVSKY, TERESA, JESUS (& PAUL)

Let me introduce you to my diverse set of friends. One of the pleasures of reading is befriending people through their work and then gathering them all together in your mind so they also befriend and converse with one another. In my mind, I have befriended and made others befriend many people they may never know, and these are friendships I cherish. And when it comes to modern humanity's holy wars over injustice and hostility, I've listened to my friends with astonishment as their varying voices converge with clarity on this point: think little, live local, love your neighbor.

In the aftermath of George Floyd's murder, many were understandably demanding big, immediate change, but if America does indeed have a *systemic* race problem (and I think it is obvious we do), that means, by definition, there is no such thing as a big, immediate fix. A systemic problem cannot be solved quickly—that's what it means for a problem to be systemic.

Former President Barack Obama, who ran on a platform of hope and change, understood this and penned a short essay responding to Floyd's murder that received little attention, mostly because it was so stone-cold sober. If you're outraged by Floyd's murder, and believe policing needs reform, then spend less time obsessing over national politics and more time tending neighborhood politics—*your* neighborhood's politics:

> When we think about politics, a lot of us focus only on the presidency and the federal government.... But the elected officials who matter most in reforming police departments and the criminal justice system work at the state and local levels.... Unfortunately, voter turnout in these local races is usually pitifully low, especially among young people—which makes no sense given the direct impact these offices have on social justice issues...[82]

Here is the former president of the United States, an ambassador for big change, an advocate of global responsibility, advising us that the change we seek will happen in our neighborhoods or it will not happen at all.

Earlier I mentioned Willie James Jennings, formerly the first black dean of Duke Divinity School and now a professor at Yale. His magisterial book *The Christian Imagination: Theology and the Origins of Race* is a work I will be processing for the rest of my life. A tour-de-force consideration of the complex and tragic racial history left (and still being left) in the wake of Western Christianity's colonizing spirit, the book leaves one dizzied—we are now aware the problem is worse than we thought, but we're a bit unclear what to do about it all. And having arranged such a large score, one is surprised Jennings ends the book on what appears a rather minor note:

> By attending to the spatial dynamics at play in the formation of social existence, we would be able to imagine reconfigurations of living spaces that might promote more just societies. Such living spaces may open up the possibilities of different ways of life that announce invitations for joining. Of course, our imaginations have been so conditioned by economically determined spatial strictures that increasingly different peoples do in fact live next to each other and [yet] remain profoundly isolated. Thus spatial reconfiguration must stand within a wider analysis and intervention into the ways identity formation has been channeled away from place.[83]

After framing Western Christianity's race problem in planetary dimensions, Jennings spends the last page of his book suggesting we must prioritize the creation of living spaces that encourage more just societies and announce invitations for joining, and then states this will require the ruthless rejection of modernity's pernicious tendency to channel identity formulation away from place. Translation: so long as we imagine our identities untethered from the places we actually live, we are doomed to be people who do not know how to justly be anywhere, so we must reacquire "a social imagination that begins to take place seriously."[84]

Ezra Klein is another friend I've made along the way—he's a progressive political commentator who co-founded *Vox* and is now a columnist for *The New York Times*. I've referenced his superb book *Why We're Polarized* several times, and at the end of his comprehensive consideration of America's political polarization problem, he—like Berry, Obama, and Jennings—counsels us to reduce our problems to the scale of our competence and pay attention to our actual place:

> I'll be blunt here in a way that cuts against my professional interests: we give too much attention to national politics, which we can do very little to change, and too little attention to state and local politics, where our voices can matter much more. The time spent spraying outrage over Trump's latest tweet ... is better spent checking in with what's happening in your own neighborhood.[85]

When a self-proclaimed national politics wonk like Klein concedes his field is full of sound and fury but often signifies little to nothing, I'm inclined to listen. (Arguments against self-interest are powerful things.)

My next friend died long before I was born. One of our greatest novelists and perhaps the greatest psychologist in modern history, Fyodor Dostoyevsky was a prodigious observer of humanity. And though a feature of his thought too little appreciated, Dostoyevsky often noted how easy it is to love humanity in general, and how difficult it is to love people in particular. As one of his characters in *The Brothers Karamazov* says,

> I love mankind ... but I am amazed at myself: the more I love mankind in general, the less I love people in particular. ... In my dreams ... [I] would really have gone to the cross for people if it were somehow suddenly necessary, and yet I am incapable of living in the same room with anyone for even two days. ... In twenty-four hours I can begin to hate even the best of men: one because he takes too long eating his dinner, another because he has a cold and keeps blowing his nose. I become the enemy of people the moment they touch me.[86]

While I doubt she intended as a rebuttal to Dostoyevsky's claim, Brené Brown has stated that, actually, people are hard to hate up close, so we should always move in.[87] And while appreciating Brown's intent (once we really get to know people and understand their stories, we inevitably feel empathy), we must know different people because I'm with Dostoyevsky: people are easy to hate up close.

That being so, we are constantly tempted to "love" "humanity" at a distance and so fancy ourselves champions of the grand human project, but our love of the idea of people is in fact a grand barrier to the actual love of actual people. It is no coincidence that most attempts at heroic gestures in Dostoyevsky's novels are pursued by deluded, impatient, and self-absorbed daydreamers.[88]

It is also no coincidence the moments of grace and joy that penetrate the heaviness of Dostoyevsky's novels, like flowers blooming in sidewalk cracks, are acts of fidelity and kindness of the smallest sort—"the labor of conserving life in small particulars, a commitment to human history not as a grand project but as the continuance of a vulnerable localized care."[89] It is likewise instructive that these small acts of enormous devotion are undertaken by patient, unheroic people—"the person prepared to begin with the transformation of the will itself and so attend to the smallest of local duties and demands."[90]

Then we have Mother Teresa, who is credited with saying, "If you want to bring happiness to the whole world, go home and love your family." And while she did not say this, she did say something like it in her 1979 Nobel Prize acceptance speech: "And so, my prayer for you is that truth will bring prayer in our homes, and from the foot of prayer will be that we believe that in the poor it is Christ. And we will really believe, we will begin to love . . . First in our own home, next door neighbor in the country we live, in the whole world."[91]

While the quotation is a bit tricky to follow grammatically, we gather what she means and sense the convergence: here is the most-admired person of the twentieth century, accepting the Nobel Peace Prize, and closing with an admonition to remember that love must begin in our own home. And she's preaching what she practiced because all that even Mother Teresa ever did was love the person in front of her, for love has no other form.

My final friend needs no introduction, and I suspect I need not connect these dots for anyone, but when asked which commandment is the greatest, Jesus is decisive: love God and love your neighbor (Mark 12:28–31). Interestingly, the apostle Paul further reduces Jesus' own reduction of the will of God from love of God and love of neighbor to just love of neighbor: "For the whole Law is fulfilled in one word, in the statement, 'You shall love your neighbor as yourself'" (Gal 5:14). Paul does not explain where he gets the chutzpah to abridge Jesus' greatest commandment, but his rationale is easily discerned: love of neighbor is the primary form of the love of God; love of neighbor *is* love of God.

And it is imperative we not treat this metaphorically and so suppose that in telling us to love our neighbor, Jesus and Paul are metaphorically telling us to love "all humanity." Doing so is a betrayal of the greatest commandment because (at the risk of belaboring the point) when everybody is your neighbor then nobody is your neighbor, and we end up turning Jesus' command of literal love for literal neighbors into a metaphor so we can metaphorically do it rather than literally do it.

Love your neighbor—this is the will of God, and it's not a metaphor.

A SUMMONS TO STABILITY

Church is a place we learn to love God, which is to say, a place we learn to love our neighbor. This is the most difficult of all lessons, which is why we noted that Calvin considered the church a gym and should also note that Saint Benedict believed his monastic community was a workshop where people learned to shape holy lives using the tools gifted to us by Christ.

Rowan Williams has brilliantly explored Benedict's communal vision in *The Way of St Benedict* and points out that Benedict's Rule is, at its heart, a summons to stability. Benedict understood transience makes holiness impossible—a difficult word for modern people to receive: "The Rule of Benedict is . . . all about stability . . . all about staying in the same place with the same people. The height of self-denial, the extreme of asceticism, is not hair shirts and all-night vigils; it's standing next to the same person quietly for years on end."[92]

Holiness is standing next to the same person quietly for years on end.

How so? Because holiness is delicate in the sense that it requires great vulnerability, and that vulnerability is not granted unless it rests upon shared communal promises of constancy and stability. When I have promised to stand beside you for years on end, and you have promised the same, we are finally free to entrust ourselves to one another. We can put down our weapons of deception and pick up the tools of holiness, which we will need because standing next to someone quietly for years does not mean passivity, but an active commitment to their good, and in Calvin's vision of the church as a gym, this commitment will involve sparring too. We can live with patience and honesty instead of duplicity and fear because we know nobody is going anywhere. As Williams says it, "We have a lifetime for this.... No one is going to run away; and the resources of the community are there on my behalf."[93]

We have a lifetime for this. Nobody is going anywhere.

This lovely (and exceedingly biblical) thought has a severe downside: all those people we wish *would* go somewhere—somewhere else. The notion that the only thing standing between us and the kingdom come are those incorrigible people we righteously loathe is certainly irresistible, but probably a bit satanic. All things told, no, everything wouldn't be all better if we could only banish our bothersome people, but regardless that's not an option because the world will always be filled with people we dislike, and when the kingdom does come in full glory, it will be too.

Benedict knew this, and made his monks endure the crucible of stability so as to rid them of the temptation of imagining all would be well if only "they" would go away. Again commenting on Benedict's stubborn but sage realism, Williams asserts,

> A great deal of our politics, our ecclesiastical life, often our personal life as well, is dominated by the assumption that everything would be all right if only some people would go away.... But [for Benedict] ... other people are not going to go away; and therefore the heart of the spiritual challenge is how we live with that otherness—honestly, constructively, hopefully, and not blindly.[94]

The people you loathe are not going anywhere.

I am attempting to raise two wonderful but heedlessly competitive little boys, separated by just enough age to make the competition both ceaseless and ceaselessly tilted in favor of the older, and thus (almost) comically vicious. Were they born in an earlier, meaner age, one of them would not have been long for the earth. After one of their many fights, both demanded the other be banished from the family, with one plunging the rhetorical dagger particularly deep: "I'd rather have the devil for a brother! Oh wait—I already do!" A veteran of many years of brother combat myself, I weighed the petitions carefully, but banishment is hard to get away with these days, so I delivered the bad news: they would be stuck as brothers for the rest of their days. And given that neither was going anywhere, they should perhaps stop viewing their relationship as a battle to be either won or lost.

When asked why we must be careful about censoring hate speech, Ira Glasser, long-time president of the ACLU, points out that giving the government permission to censor the speech we hate at a certain point in time also means giving it permission to censor our speech should the wind of public sentiment or political power ever change, as it always does. He contends that the best response to something like the thinly veiled white-supremacist speech that became pervasive in the time of Trump was not censorship, but the election; the solution to the white-supremacist rhetoric stoked by Trump was to vote him out of office.[95]

What Glasser doesn't acknowledge is that while voting Trump out of office does not do nothing, it does little to heal the racial wound deep at the heart of American culture. After all, the embers of racist sentiment survived eight years of America's first black president and immediately flared up given some oxygen. Elections, *especially* national ones, do far less than we'd hope to solve our hate problems. We cannot vote, shame, mock, or scold away the people we dislike.

In summary, there are no shortcuts to God's joyful justice, and its form cannot take firm shape without the formation of virtue—not just personal virtue, but communal virtue. And while the formation of communal virtue involves many things, it *requires* stability. If Benedict's workshop has a product, it is the making of people who are *there*[96]—people fully present to the square foot of dirt they occupy, people fully responsible for the good of the person in the square foot of dirt beside them, people who know how to be where they are.

THE THIRST FOR AN IMMEDIATE DEED

I would apologize for invoking Wendell Berry again, but it would be insincere. For those unacquainted with him, Berry is a world-renowned essayist, novelist, and poet who was awarded the National Humanities Medal by then-President Barack Obama, but he takes far more pride in being a crotchety, small-time Kentucky farmer. A professor at the prestigious NYU at an early age, Berry found himself at the center of the literary world with no limits in sight, which was his cue to leave. He resigned from NYU, took a job at the University of Kentucky, and bought a small farm in Henry County, Kentucky, the place of his birth, and has lived there ever since. One might say all Berry's work is an exploration of this decision to live a small life in a small place.

According to Berry, modernity has a habit of creating placeless people—people who don't know how to be where they are. He tells a story about a group of early Kentucky settlers who set out to build a road in

1797.[97] They felled countless ancient trees, and when cold nights came, they made raging bonfires to stay warm and then entertained themselves by fighting with firebrands, a recreation that, predictably, ended with no small amount of violence.

He then contrasts these settlers with the Native Americans who had lived in the land for ages with so little abuse of it, who warmed small shelters with small fires using small amounts of wood on cold nights instead of hacking down ancient forests to make unnecessarily large fires just because they could. The problem with the road builders is that they were placeless people who had in no meaningful sense "arrived" in America and thus lacked the devotion and knowledge necessary to inhabit it without ruining it: "Because they belonged to no place, it was almost inevitable that they should behave violently toward the places they came to."[98]

Relating this story to his decision to leave New York City for Henry County, Kentucky, Berry says he didn't know how to be there (New York) because, in a literal and existential sense, it was not where he was from. He could not avoid acting like a tourist and critic there—like a rock skipping across the surface of its life, seeing problems for which he could not conjure up a sense of responsibility. So he found a place he could be and has spent the rest of his life learning how to be there.

He also does an inordinate amount of talking about topsoil because there's "no use talking about getting enlightened or saving your soul if you can't keep the topsoil from washing away."[99] This is and isn't a metaphor. One can be forgiven for not knowing this fact, but topsoil is essential for healthy crops, and healthy crops are essential for a healthy humanity, and it takes around fifty thousand years for nature to make a mere five feet of topsoil. This slow recipe is becoming an immanent problem because around half of earth's topsoil has been lost over the last 150 years, implying our current course is a dead end.

Let me risk disappointing the stubbornly literal Berry with a metaphorical move: humanity's topsoil, especial in the "civilized" world, seems to be eroding at a rate similar to earth's. Our desire to think big, live big, and be from everywhere has mostly meant we are people from nowhere who do not know how to be here, which means we erode wherever we are with our non-present presence. And it is a large problem made larger by the introduction of large solutions.

But like Berry, I offer no large solutions because there are none: "There is . . . a conspicuous shortage of large-scale corrections for problems that have large-scale causes. . . . I don't think there are solutions commensurate with our problems. I think the great problems call for many small solutions."[100] And I can think of no better image of the hope local churches can offer the world than that of being places where we learn to be people who are here, places where topsoil slowly accumulates so that God's joyful justice might take root and grow into a crop that grows into a feast for the world.

The image is also quite boring. We don't want to be told the best we can do is submit to the plodding process by which we're made into good dirt so that something greater than ourselves can grow. Who has time for that? Who aspires to be topsoil? Speaking of the desire (most typical among young men) to do something sensational, Dostoyevsky observes the naiveté wherein a youth is genuinely willing to sacrifice life itself for a spectacular action but unwilling to commit himself to a long formation in virtue that will turn him into a person with more to offer the world than one spectacular sacrifice:

> These young men do not understand that the sacrifice of life is, perhaps the easiest of all sacrifices in many cases, while to sacrifice, for example, five or six years of their ebulliently youthful life to hard, difficult studies, to learning, in order to increase tenfold their strength to serve the very truth and the very deed that they loved. . . . [S]uch sacrifice is quite often almost beyond the strength of many of them.[101]

He calls this "the thirst for an immediate deed," and modern people know it well. The angry mob of men storming the Capitol and saving the country had a thirst for the immediate deed. But we must not be too proud for refusing to join their ranks because the thirst for it wells up in us all, and often. Hauerwas adds his voice to this choir when he advocates "the grace of doing one thing," by which he means we must stop thinking we must do everything or nothing, and instead "take the time to do one thing that might help lead myself and others to God's peace . . . for that 'one thing' is just enough to remove us from the familiar world of violence so that our imagination might be freed to find yet one other thing we might do."[102]

At the beginning of *Spider-Man: Far From Home*, Peter Parker is basking in the warm glow of celebrity. He has helped reverse a catastrophic extinction event, in which the alien Thanos had "snapped" half of all life in the universe out of existence. But while he's a hero basking in the glow of celebrity, he's also a reluctant celebrity because, unlike many heroes, Peter

Parker is not a galactic hero; he's your friendly neighborhood Spider-Man. And so while being peppered with big questions about his place in the interdimensional superhero hierarchy and contingency plans for future alien invasions, Spider-Man responds with a question of his own: "Does anyone have any neighborhood questions?"[103] Sounds like Spider-Man reads Wendell Berry.

Writing in a time devoid of world wars and internal campaigns to make Israel great again, the prophet Zechariah called this period of Israel's history "the day of small things" and warned people to dare not despise it: "For who has despised the day of small things?" (Zech 4:10). Jesus riffs on this when he says, "If then you cannot do even a very little thing, why do you worry about other matters?" (Luke 12:26). Paul continues the theme: "Make it your ambition to lead a quiet life . . ." (1 Thess 4:11).

We are again, and in truth always are, in the day of small things, but we dare not despise it. Unable, according to Jesus, to do even a very little thing, do then the *very, very* little thing that is yours to do. Before you storm the Capitol, teach your children to pray. Before you save the country, break bread with your neighbor. Before you make America just, make your community more just. Before you imagine yourself responsible for the world, responsibly submit to and serve your household of faith. Before you compose a grand opera, play your part well in the simple tune of the gospel.

The last word on this must go to Berry, and his "pleasingly unoriginal" formula for a good life and good community: "Slow down. Pay attention. Do good work. Love your neighbors. Love your place. Stay in your place. Settle for less, enjoy it more."[104]

5

Clashing Victimocracies
We (Not They) Are Causing the Crisis

IN 2017, A YOUNG, award-winning Swedish journalist named Kim Wall boarded a small, homemade submarine for a hastily scheduled interview with a locally famous inventor—a man who turned out to be a sadist who killed her and dumped her remains in the ocean. *The Investigation* is the name of the six-episode HBO miniseries that explores her tragic murder and the resulting investigation into it, and at the end of its six-plus-hours running time we realize that the (seemingly) most crucial detail of the story has been glossed: we never meet the killer; we never hear his name. Why? In two words, *because Jesus*.

Two millennia ago, Jesus of Nazareth stands before Pontius Pilate. History tells us how this story will end—Pilate will bow and break Christ—and history ensures this is how the story will be told: mighty Pilate remembered, the carpenter's son forgotten. This is Pilate's story because history and the telling of it revolves around main characters like Pilate. Indeed, this *is* history—remembering and celebrating the names and deeds of men like Pilate. But this will no longer be history because deep in the bowels of creation something tectonic has occurred, as portended by the Easter-morn earthquake. History and the telling of it will no longer revolve around Pilates, but instead around this most unimportant man: the Nazarene.

Thus says David Bentley Hart,

> Told aright, the true story is first and foremost the story of those that human memory has accorded no names: the poor, the rejected, the despised, the enslaved. These abandoned persons, more or less exclusively, are the whole center of a proper Christian understanding of the past, and so of a proper Christian desire for the future. Though they have been deprived of their names, God has given them the name of Christ; though they have been forgotten, he has given them Christ's story as their own. Where they are, he is present; and, in human history, he is most truly present *nowhere else*. And so the Christian narrative should be a constant and subversive counternarrative, a ceaseless interruption and riposte.[105]

Living so far downstream from this founding event, it is perhaps inevitable the apocalyptic absurdity of it is mostly lost on us. The fact that Jesus and not Pilate is the main character in the telling of Jesus' story as we have learned to tell it tells us just how totalizing the crucifixion and resurrection truly were. Though their effects are variously delayed and resisted, there is a rather irresistible sense in which it now occurs to us to tell the story of history from the bottom, to stand on our heads if we wish to see things as God does. And, again, this upside-down telling of history occurs to us, not because of "reason" or "the Enlightenment" or "empathy" or "human rights" or "social justice," but because God raised Jesus from the dead and re-founded the world on the story of the unimportant person crucified by all the important people.

And so, two thousand years later, a previously unthinkable thought is now thinkable, and a Danish screenwriter and director imagines telling the story of the murder of Kim Walsh as the story of Kim Walsh while giving her killer the forgotten face and nameless name he deserves. It is a variation of a story we once did not know how to tell but now find it difficult not to tell: the story of the victory of the victim over the victor; the story God told the world in Christ.

The attraction of this story for modern people is immense, and history's most modern man, Friedrich Nietzsche, was unhappy about it. Though a viciously atheistic philosopher, Nietzsche had a better grasp on Christianity that many Christians and correctly discerned that Christianity (when faithful to Christ) ruins history by banishing heroes and celebrating slaves. It replaces classic, muscular heroism with a "slave morality" that makes virtues of unvirtuous, pusillanimous vices like meekness, humility, and empathy. It bows and breaks Pilate before Christ.

As a prophet for a severe but lucid anti-humanistic atheism, Nietzsche's disdain for Christianity's story of the victory of the victim over the victor makes complete sense. What does not make sense is the tendency for many modern Christians to side in large part with Nietzsche and betray the story that God told the world in Christ by refusing to discern the story of history from the bottom, by becoming relentlessly critical of victim narratives. Because Christians are theologically obligated to be drawn to victim narratives. If you're a Christian repelled by victim narratives, you're a Christian who has forgotten your story.

Channeling the work of liberation theologians who have themselves channeled the teaching of Scripture, Miroslav Volf says the same thing from the opposite angle:

> For those who appeal to the biblical traditions, the presumption that one perspective is as valid as the other until proven otherwise is unacceptable. The initial suspicion against the perspective of the powerful is necessary. Not because the powerless are innocent, but because the powerful have the means to impose their own perspective by argument and propaganda. . . . The Jewish prophets—and indeed the whole of the Scriptures—are biased toward the powerless. Such a preferential option for the powerless implies a privileged hearing for those whose voices are excluded, the so-called "epistemological privilege of the oppressed."[106]

With this foreword in place and always in view, we're in a better place to navigate our odd cultural moment wherein the story of the victory of victims over victors is currently under an enormous amount of (what the philosopher Charles Taylor calls) cross-pressure, being both claimed and criticized from every direction, allegedly meaning everything and nothing and many things in between.

HONOR, DIGNITY, VICTIMHOOD

Most kingdoms throughout history—be they animal or human—have been, in their own idiosyncratic ways, *honor cultures*, meaning worth is conferred based upon reputation, and reputation is gained by forcibly flexing and defending one's dominance. When someone strikes you on the cheek in an honor culture, you have a moral imperative to strike back and strike back harder. Failure to do so is a moral failure resulting in a loss of reputation, status, and honor. You make yourself less worthy when you fail to defend and demonstrate your honor.

Some part of that dominate-or-be-dominated instinct remains in your lizard brain, but if you're reading this book, there's a good chance you're ill at ease with it. While the vestiges of honor culture are still present in the modern world (think gangs or extremist groups or our obsession with revenge-centric entertainment), it has in large part been eclipsed by what we might call *dignity cultures*, and in dignity cultures worth is internally possessed and not externally bestowed, is grounded in personal dignity and not prevailing public opinion. In contradistinction to honor cultures, in dignity cultures you are weak and unworthy if obsessed with your reputation, and you make yourself even less worthy when you strike back because your retaliation is merely a display of your insecurity and barbarism.

Obviously the offspring of a Christian moral heritage, dignity culture is the dominant form of culture in the West, and one of its great strengths is its capacity to create people whose profound sense of inner dignity makes them less susceptible (though certainly not impervious) to slights, insults, litigiousness, self-pity, and retaliatory violence.

In their book *The Rise of Victimhood Culture*, Bradley Campbell and Jason Manning trace the genealogy of Western moral culture(s) as they moved from an exclusive emphasis on honor, to an increasing emphasis on dignity, to the newest evolution: a growing emphasis on victimhood.[107] In victimhood cultures, victimhood is a moral virtue that confers worth upon the victim and her allies. Demonstrations of one's oppression and the oppressors' iniquity, or one's commitment to amplify the victim's oppression and the oppressors' iniquity, is a means to both external (honor) and internal (dignity) worth. Thus, in *The Madness of Crowds* Douglas Murray notes that "Victimhood rather than stoicism or heroism has become something eagerly publicized, even sought after, in our culture."[108]

Similarly, in *Cynical Theories*, Helen Pluckrose and James Lindsay unpack the history of the cluster of ideologies (postcolonial, queer, feminist, race, gender) that are part of a general ideological family of critical theories, united in their desire to organize the world around favored (victim) and unfavored (oppressor) groups. They specifically highlight the work of Edward Said, a Palestinian-American theorist and the father of postcolonial theory, who was, they say, one of the first to forcibly attempt to "rewrite history from the perspective of the oppressed."[109]

Writing from a classic liberal perspective, these authors represent a growing pushback to critical theory in its various expressions. Classic liberals seem to have reached a consensus that critical theories are too prone to subvert reason in the name of social justice by means of increasingly niche identity structures that become over-determining epistemological themes. While this phenomenon is an interesting intramural quarrel within the liberal camp, what must most strike a Christian is the general failure of Christian faithfulness evidenced by the fact that someone could claim that a twentieth-century postcolonial theorist writing two thousand years after Christ was, basically, the first person to rewrite history from the perspective of the oppressed.

No—the first person to rewrite history from the perspective of the oppressed was the God of Abraham, Isaac, and Jacob, the God of Israel, the God and Father of our Lord, Jesus Christ, and the first upside-down telling of history was the Bible. And shame on us that anyone could suggest otherwise.

It is an undeniable fact (even if it is prone to being denied in both hyper-conservative Christian and progressive-activist circles) that victimhood culture, with its attendant upside-down framing of the past, present, and future, is, like dignity culture, quite obviously the offspring of a Christian moral heritage. It's the sort of culture one might create if one believed Pilate and not Jesus was being judged in their infamous encounter.

On a related note, Western cultures are especially hospitable to critical theories and their emphasis on victimhood because the Western moral imagination has been fertilized by the story of the crucified God. To highlight one of the more obvious counterexamples, cultures shaped by the story of Islam are unlikely to find victim narratives nearly as compelling because Islam tells a different story. To be clear, Islam, like Christianity, is a diverse religion. It contains multitudes, and many of those multitudes bear no semblance to the Islamophobic caricatures so popular in many Western countries. But Christianity and Islam are different religions for a reason: they tell different stories. And one of the main differences in the stories they tell is that in Christianity the most high God is a murdered victim, and in Islam the most high God is not. In Christianity, reality revolves around the crucifixion—in Islam, it does not. This is not an insignificant plot divergence.

So yet again, Christians are theologically obligated to be drawn to victim narratives, and the centering of victims occurring in many corners of western culture is (even if denied by conservative Christians or unacknowledged by liberal scholars and progressive activists) a Christian phenomenon—a tremor rippling across history from the epicenter that is the crucifixion and resurrection of the son of God.

I have delayed the *but* until now because many Christians are criticizing modern social justice movements and the critical theories underlying them with a sinfully critical spirit posing as critical thinking, and that is the most critical observation for Christians to make. *But* what does need some sorting is how Christians might preserve an explicitly Christian telling of the victim story now that it has become fashionable to tell victim stories.

THE LINE SEPARATING GOOD & EVIL

Giving up on a childhood faith he felt he'd outgrown, Aleksandr Solzhenitsyn became an evangelical atheist and Marxist as a young man. The movement back to the faith he thought he'd outgrown was set in motion when he served as a captain in the Russian Army during World War II and was sentenced to hard time in the Gulag and then exiled for criticizing Stalin. And out there in the frozen purgatory of the Russian wilds, he discovered something.

Shed all the niceties and incentives and fortuities and illusions and propaganda—venture out to the extremities of human experience—and our standard moral ideals evaporate as we are left staring down *the* cold, brute, ultimate moral truth: we are, *all of us*, good and evil. In his own words:

> Gradually it was disclosed to me that the line separating good and evil passes not through states, nor between classes, nor between political parties either—but right through every human heart—and through all human hearts. This line shifts. Inside us, it oscillates with the years. And even within hearts overwhelmed by evil, one small bridgehead of good is retained. And even in the best of all hearts, there remains ... an unuprooted small corner of evil.[110]

He had entered prison full of rage and justice and quickly descended into "aimless hate, irritability, and nervousness." And his righteous rage felt good, felt *righteous*. He pondered the moral imbecility of his oppressors, he nursed his moral superiority, but as the years passed, he found himself increasingly looking down into his own heart instead of down his nose at his oppressors, wondering, "Am I any better?"

> There is nothing that so aids and assists the awakening of omniscience within us as insistent thought about one's own transgressions, errors, mistakes. After the difficult cycles of such ponderings over many years, whenever I mentioned the heartlessness of our highest-ranking bureaucrats, the cruelty of our executioners, I remember myself in my captain's shoulder boards and the forward march of my battery through East Prussia, enshrouded in fire, and I say: "So were we any better?"[111]

His descent into self-righteous rage became an ascent into the mercy of God when he accepted that the line dividing good and evil runs right through every human heart.

Far from moral relativity, this is moral lucidity and a bedrock affirmation of basic biblical anthropology. It is the basis of the colossal "all-sides-ing" Paul does in Romans (which we'll explore later). Everyone has sinned. Everyone is a sinner. God owes no one anything. Do you imagine you are better than someone else? Perhaps you are, but would you be if you had lived their life? What if you had their genes, their biology, their body, their brain chemistry? Still think you'd be better? And even if you *are* better than someone else, perhaps that entitles you to certain perks in the world as we know it, but what exactly does that entitle you to before your maker? Nothing—at least according to Paul.

Inviting judgmental Jews and condescending gentiles around a common table, Paul reminds these early Christian churches located at the heart of the Roman Empire that they've been gathered together as a family by the God who justifies the ungodly. Paul reminds them that God's family is constituted by the ungodly and not the godly. Paul reminds them that accepting one's acceptance into God's family is accepting that one has been accepted as one who is ungodly and not because one is godly.

And this is the reminder central to the stewardship of an explicitly Christian telling of the victim story: the victim *par excellence* is not us, but Christ. *We* crucified *him*! And before any other Christian riff on the victim story may be told, the original story must have its say: the son of God is the victim, we are the perps.

This claim is a tough sell in modern circles. God a victim? Please. God—if he or she or it exists—is the creator of our awful and unjust world, so if there is a victim to be found, it is surely us and not God. This mood pervades modernity, so much so that even among modern believers there's a tendency to see ourselves primarily as victims who suffer and not sinners who sin.

And of course it is true that we are victims who suffer, and the modern theological emphasis on Christ our fellow sufferer is a most welcome and faithful accentuation of the crucifixion story, but when humanity-the-victim eclipses Christ-the-victim, the story has become perverted. Before the crucifixion can become the more general story of the victory of the victim over the victor, it must be the particular story of the crucified God—of our betrayal swallowed up by the son of God's fidelity on a Roman cross around 33 AD.

Lamenting the activist tendency to divide the world into "us" and "them," Wendell Berry does some all-sides-ing that would make the apostle Paul proud. After chiding environmental activist for self-congratulatory grandstanding, he challenges all of us to get down to the real business at hand:

> *We* are causing the crisis. Nearly every one of us, nearly every day of his life, is contributing directly to the ruin of this planet. A protest meeting on the issue of environmental abuse is not a convocation of accusers; it is a convocation of the guilty. That realization ought to clear the smog of self-righteousness that has almost conventionally hovered over these occasions and let us see the work that is to be done.[112]

They are not causing the crisis. *We* are. *I* am. The primary problem for which I am responsible is me, not them. So if we are to gather in the pursuit of God's joyful justice done on earth as it is in heaven, we must first and foremost understand our gathering as a convocation of the guilty. Before we dare to claim that we stand with and for Christ, we must first confess that we have stood against him, and still do, and far more often than we'd care to admit.

CAN YOU EMBRACE A CETNIK?

Few have explored our shared culpability better than Miroslav Volf. In his prescient and award-winning book *Exclusion and Embrace*, he attempts to complement the pursuit of social justice uniquely present in liberation theology with "a theology of embrace."[113] He recounts the famed theologian Jürgen Moltmann asking him, "Can you embrace a *cetnik*?"

Having just argued that we ought to embrace our enemies as Christ embraced us, Volf was taken aback by Moltmann's question because *cetniks* were the infamous Serbian fighters who were brutalizing people in Volf's native country, Croatia. They herded people into concentration camps, raped women, burned churches. Should they really be embraced? Volf found himself torn in two by his own faith:

> My thought was pulled in two different directions by the blood of the innocent crying out to God and the blood of God's Lamb offered for the guilty. How does one remain loyal both to the demand of the oppressed for justice and to the gift of forgiveness that the Crucified offered to the perpetrators? . . . I felt that my very faith was at odds with itself, divided . . . between the demand to bring about justice for the victims and the call to embrace the perpetrator.[114]

As mentioned earlier, this is the justice/friendship tension that lies uniquely at the heart of Christian faith, a tension we must play instead of exorcize, and Volf plays it as well as it can be played. He concedes no ground to injustice—it cannot be cheaply covered up in the name of forgiveness; repentance necessitates restitution. Like little Zacchaeus, we who have oppressed and defrauded others must not simply apologize, but do what we can to make it right—give away half our possessions, pay back four times what we stole, whatever it takes (Luke 19:8).

And while not a qualification, we must also affirm that Jesus came calling *everyone* to repentance. Volf acknowledges many have an understandable struggle with this part of Jesus' teaching. While ferociously critical of unjust oppressors, Jesus had no qualms calling the poor, the sad, and the victimized to repentance as well. Furthermore, it is disingenuous to claim that repentance for oppressors meant, well, repentance, but for victims it meant embracing hope and dignity: "Nothing suggests such a categorizing of people in Jesus' ministry, though different people ought to repent of different kinds of sins."[115] Agreeing with Volf, Esau McCaulley makes a complementary observation in *Reading While Black*:

> It is important to point out that the "gospel" preached here does more than affirm the value of the poor. Jesus sees them as *moral agents* capable of repentance. . . . His call to repentance acknowledges the fact that their poverty doesn't remove their agency. The poor are capable of sin and repentance.[116]

Why would Jesus be so harsh to the poor and oppressed? Does repentance really need to be piled on top of their towering burden of poverty and oppression? As always, Jesus' apparent severity is only a means to mercy, and he insists that even victims repent for the most merciful of reasons.

First, envy and enmity are constant temptations when one has been chronically wronged, and no matter how justifiable envy and enmity are, they are poison. Envy and enmity lock victims into a perverse communion with oppressors, so victims must repent of envy and enmity if they are to be truly free of their oppressors:

> Victims need to repent of the fact that all too often they mimic the behavior of the oppressors, let themselves be shaped in the mirror image of their enemy.... Though victims may not be able to prevent hate from springing to life, for their own sake they can and must refuse to give it nourishment and strive to weed it out. If victims do not repent today they will become perpetrators tomorrow.[117]

Victims need to repent because it is an essential step in their personal journey out of victimization and into liberation.

Additionally, victims need to repent not just for their own personal sake, but also for society's sake, for the world's sake. Acknowledging that the categories of victim/oppressor are indispensable, Volf asserts, "we must resist making them the overarching schema by which to align our social engagement."[118] Why? Because it's ill-suited to bring about justice and friendship in societies because if "the plot is written around the schema of 'oppressed' and 'oppressors,' each party will find good reasons for claiming the higher moral ground of a victim; each will perceive itself as oppressed by the other and all will see themselves as engaged in the struggle for liberation."[119]

Peter Leithart calls it the problem of "clashing victimocracies"—a stupendously accurate description of the current American political scene: "Elite brokers take up the cause of favored victims, while Trumpism inverts the victimocracy by teaching Middle American whites to see themselves as victims of elites and their clients. On the streets of Portland, aggrieved antifa activists battle aggrieved patriots with fists and baseball bats."[120]

Coming from a much more progressive angle, even Ezra Klein concedes, "American politics is often a chorus of contradictory voices persuasively claiming victimhood at the same time."[121] Rabbi Jonathan Sacks frames it as a battle between identity-politics progressives and populist conservatives where everyone loses because we "lose our feeling of collective responsibility and find in its place a culture of competitive victimhood."[122]

Or as Dave Chappelle, one of the most perceptive commentators on the American social scene, sees it, we all appear to be competing in the "Discrimination Olympics," vying for the title of the most discriminated against as a means to being the greatest.[123] Tell the story of victim and oppressor as if it's the only story to tell and people will find a way to tell that story, both to themselves and others, to their advantage.

As a point of clarification, it's probably important to note that while critiques of victimhood culture have tended to be levelled by conservatives at progressives, it seems conservatives are every bit as guilty of aiding and abetting it as progressives. Progressives certainly don't have a monopoly on crying wolf, and conservatives know how to spin the tale of themselves as victim as well as anyone. Just observe how conservative Christian nationalists weep and wail and cry out to almighty God for justice because football players are kneeling during the national anthem and they've lost their grip on being the most powerful political group in the most powerful nation in the history of the world.

So Jesus calls everyone, victims included, to repent because it's essential for the healing of both victims and societies. But all pragmatic considerations aside, Jesus ultimately calls everyone to repent because the line dividing good and evil runs right through every human heart, which is to say that Jesus calls everyone to repent because everyone needs to repent. After all, Jesus does not stand with victims because they are innocent; Jesus stands with victims because they are victims.

Sounding the rumbling bass note at the heart of the biblical story, Volf contends that sealed divisions between victims and oppressors exist in theory and certain specific situations, but not in *life, writ large*: "It is simply not the case that one can construe narratives of the encounter between parties in conflict as stories of manifest evil on the one side and indisputable good on the other."[124]

In his masterpiece *Resurrection*, Rowan Williams comes to a similar conclusion. In life as it actually is, the boundary between victim and oppressor is maddeningly fluid. You can be victim one moment, oppressor the next. You can be victim and oppressor in the same moment! You can be the condemned Christ in one relationship, Pilate condemning Christ in another. Though we long for clean lines, "The human world is not one of clearly distinguishable bodies of oppressors and victims, those who inflict damage and those who bear it. Where is a 'pure victim' to be found?"[125]

Though we like to pretend that matters of victim and oppression, of blame and justice, of good and bad, of right and wrong, are exercises in simple moral accounting, there are enormous unknown integers in most all the equations, so we should stop pretending we're doing elementary moral math. And besides being ignorant moral accountants, we're also crooked accountants—always placing a finger on the scale, always inserting a few of our own lines when claiming to speak for God.

In his remarkably even-handed treatment of black liberation theology, Anthony Bradley, himself an African American theologian, affirms the systemic oppression of blacks by whites that serves as one of America's founding sins, but then also adds that "there is not a people group on earth that has not, at some point, been both the oppressed and the oppressor."[126] And so on grounds of biblical anthropology, Bradley suggests that victimhood must not, even for those who are indeed victims, become "an overcontrolling theme."[127] It's a note that must be struck and struck often in many contexts, but it cannot be the bass line.

So we must be wary of categorical, pure construals that portray people and groups as pure victims and pure oppressors, because while such construals may be true of *particular situations*, they are false of *life* and incongruent with basic biblical anthropology. We must categorically reject all categorical construals except Scripture's totalizing affirmation that all are (beloved) sinners.

As Rowan Williams asks, where is a pure victim to be found? Nowhere—with one exception: Christ. And as the one pure victim, Christ judges all oppression and injustice. As the one pure victim, Christ judges our justice. But in judging our justice, Williams points out that Christ neither condemns nor inverts it.[128] Instead, Christ *transcends* our justice in the creation of a new humanity no longer locked in petty power struggles between aspiring tyrants. Christ invites us to imagine and inhabit a world where powerful vs. powerless power struggles are antiquated because, like our master, we exist not to be served but to serve. Christ insists that just as friendship without justice is not truly friendship, so justice without friendship is not truly justice.

So on personal, social, biblical, and theological grounds, there is no future in the clash of victimocracies, and we must pursue a transcendent justice that does justice to the friendly, joyful justice known as the gospel. How?

KEEPING OUR BROTHERS & SISTERS & SELVES

Absorbed as we understandably are in our particular moment, voices from a different time and place can help us see angles we are too close to see, and we are wise to again call upon the services of Dostoyevsky, Saint Benedict (with another assist from Roman Williams), and the apostle Paul.

Best known for his explorations of God, suffering, and evil, Dostoyevsky had an equally keen sense for issues of justice and responsibility. Lying on his deathbed, the character Father Zosima spends most of his final moments reflecting on the biblical imperative to be a person who takes responsibility for others—all others:

> There is only one salvation for you: take yourself up, and make yourself responsible for all the sins of men. For . . . the moment you make yourself sincerely responsible for everything and everyone, you will see at once that it is really so, that it is you who are guilty on behalf of all and for all.[129]

These last remarks are anticipated earlier in the book as well:

> But when [a man] knows that he is not only worse than all those in the world, but is also guilty before all people, on behalf of all and for all, for all human sins, the world's and each person's, only then will the goal of our unity be achieved. For you must know, my dear ones, that each of us is undoubtedly guilty on behalf of all and for all on earth . . .[130]

Surely this is absurd! Make yourself responsible for the sins of all people? In the previous chapter we discussed the silliness of imaging oneself heroically responsible for the whole world. But notice the difference: Dostoyevsky is not here suggesting we are responsible for fixing the whole world, but that *instead of* imaging ourselves responsible for fixing the whole world, we must confess that we (not *them*) have broken the world and cannot fix it. We are not responsible for fixing the world, but we are responsible for breaking it, confessing it, and, by the Spirit, mending it as it presents itself to us (primarily in the form of our neighbor).

In Dostoyevsky's vision, life is an ocean wherein all things flow and connect to each other, where we touch in one place and it "echoes at the other end of the world."[131] And in such a world, it's not feigning humility to confess that our sins ricochet, replicate, and reproduce wantonly across creation *forever*. Even when standing before a criminal, he dares us to entertain the notion that "if I myself were righteous, perhaps there would be no criminal standing before me now."[132] Even when surrounded by spiteful and calloused people who will not give you a hearing, "fall down before them and ask their forgiveness, for the guilt is yours, too, that they do not want to listen to you."[133]

Charles Taylor thus observes the slogan of all Dostoyevsky's villains is "no one is to blame," whereas the slogan of his heroes is "we are all to blame," and the miracle of healing comes upon us only when we accept rather than avoid responsibility.[134]

Following in the wake of this cosmic vision of the responsibility of all for the sin and guilt of all, two things beg clarification. First, Dostoyevsky is at pains to demonstrate that such a magnanimous posture is impossible, but it is an impossibility made possible when one comes to know the height and depth and width and breadth of the love of God. When you have received the gift of your eternal and boundless beloved-ness, you are free to accept responsibility for the sins of all without shame or despair. You can fearlessly and even joyfully accept culpability because you have nothing to lose and nothing to gain—all has already been given to you freely in Christ.

It's no coincidence that most all the great liturgical traditions invite us to start our days by reminding ourselves of our beloved-ness and then confessing our sins. The order is important.

I've found few practices more transformative than receiving God's love and then boldly confessing my sins to start the day. Because then as the day proceeds and I do something sinful or stupid, my inner defense attorney leaps into action arguing for my innocence, but then the Spirit gently reminds him the defense has already rested its case for the day. The charges are all true! Guilty as charged—guilty, but loved, and that is enough. As Volf says, "Whether we are aggressors or victims, genuine repentance demands that we . . . refuse to explain our behavior and accuse others, and simply take our wrongdoing upon ourselves."[135] Besides, I've got better things to do than defend myself—that's Jesus' job, and he's quite good at it. Relieved of that burden, I'm free to spend my day more productively, gladly taking responsibility for the sin and suffering around me instead of telling myself and everyone who will listen that it's not my problem.

Second, Dostoyevsky's insistence that we make ourselves responsible for the sins of all does not mean we make others irresponsible. We do not take responsibility for others' sins so they don't have to, but rather our taking of responsibility for others' sins often takes the form of helping others learn how to take responsibility for themselves and their sins in healthy ways. Summarizing Dostoyevsky as only he can, Rowan Williams puts it this way: "the taking of responsibility for the other . . . involves the responsibility of making responsibility possible for the other, not merely a resigned acceptance of the other's load.... Taking up the cross with and for another is not a removal of responsibility from the other; rather the contrary."[136]

So we shoulder the sins of others in a manner that beckons them to a place where they can shoulder their own sin without shame or despair because they realize their sin has all already been shouldered by Christ. And this—holding yourself responsible for making responsibility possible for those who struggle with it, without condemnation or condescension—is another impossibility made possible in Christ.

Williams' brief but luminous treatment of the Rule of Saint Benedict also contains resources to deliver us from the clash of victimocracies. He emphasizes the premium Benedict placed on transparency and genuine conflict resolution, how Benedict hated false peace. Concerned as we are with justice, modern people hate false peace too, but Williams deftly parses out how the modern hatred of false peace differs from Benedict's. He sets the scene thus:

> It's all quite difficult for us in the twenty-first century. We have been told—rightly—that it is bad to deny and repress emotion; equally right, that it is poisonous for us to be passive under injustice. The problem ... is that we so readily take this reasonable corrective to an atmosphere of unreality and oppression as an excuse for promoting the dramas of the will. The denial of emotion is a terrible thing; what takes time is learning that the positive path is the education of emotion, not its uncritical indulgence.... Likewise, the denial of rights is a terrible thing; and what takes time to learn is that the opposite of oppression is not a wilderness of litigation and reparation but the nurture of concrete, shared respect...[137]

A wilderness of litigation and reparation that promotes the dramas of the will—that's Williams' assessment of our scene, and he coins the term "audit culture" to describe it. In an audit culture, we constantly audit others to determine whether they have upheld their responsibilities to us. The moral burden is always theirs. Have they done enough to merit my forgiveness? Do they deserve communion? Have they done enough to make things right? If not, then we dare not reconcile because such reconciliation would be an unjust, false peace.

While sharing our hatred of false peace, Benedict challenges us to put the moral burden on ourselves and not them. Rather than auditing others, he asks his monks to first audit themselves:

> The warning against false peace suggests that being wary of facile reconciliation is not about a suspicion of whether the other has adequately made reparation but about whether I have fully acknowledged and dealt with my own resentment. It is a hesitation over my honesty about peace, not the other's acceptability...[138]
>
> So being wary of facile reconciliation is not just being suspicious of whether someone else has adequately done justice to me. I need to acknowledge and deal with my own bewilderment, my own resentment, so that there is a degree of hesitation in me—not about the acceptability of the peace offered by another, but about the honesty and depth and integrity of my own desire for peace and willingness to work for it.[139]

Affirming the refusal to slip into corrupt and collusive passivity, Williams also affirms Benedict's commitment to break his monks of habits of mind and action that always place the moral burden on others and so hypnotize us into a self-referential neurosis where we're chronically obsessing over whether we're being tended to as we deserve.

Such a state—audit culture—locks us into ways of being together where grievance is the primary currency, where whomever is most aggrieved is king, and turns us into people who, to quote Peggy Noonan, are proud of their bitterness.[140] There is no future here, and, once again, it falls to the church to be a society that shows society what life can look like when grievance is taken out of circulation (instead of stoked), and replaced with humility, repentance, and mutual responsibility.

Like justice, responsibility is a concept currently in dispute. With minimal hyperbole, one might observe that progressives think conservatives should be held responsible for all that ills anyone who is not a conservative, whereas conservatives think everyone should only be responsible for themselves. In isolation, both groups' beliefs are biblically irresponsible, but in collaboration there is promise, which brings us to Scripture in general, and then the apostle Paul in particular.

It is difficult to come up with a more unbiblical notion than that we are responsible only for ourselves. From beginning to end, Scripture implores us to be the keepers of our brothers and sisters, especially those who, for whatever reasons, need help. Much of the Old Testament is an attempt to help Israel set herself apart among the nations as a nation where the poor and forgotten are resourced and remembered. Israel was to take responsibility for the struggles of her least because this is what God has done for Israel—indeed, God chose Israel because she was the least (Deut

7). As such, God evaluates Israel's faithfulness to him primarily in terms of whether Israel is making herself responsible for those most in need of justice and mercy.

This extends into the New Testament. When dusk sets on a crowd of hungry people, the disciples suggest that Jesus send them away to find food and fend for themselves. Jesus' response is straight out of the Old Testament: "No, you give them something to eat" (Mark 6:37). The New Testament letters are littered with the "one-anothers"—commands to serve one another, encourage one another, build up one another, be hospitable to one another, give preference to one another, wait for one another, love one another, and most apropos, to bear one another's burdens. And this mutual sharing of burdens is not merely psychological sympathy, is not just feeling sad that someone else is struggling. Rather, the bearing of one another's burdens is taking responsibility for one another's struggles, be they spiritual, emotional, social, or economic.

And to return to the theme of the previous chapter, the primary realm of this responsibility must be, for a Christian, the church (Gal 6:10). For if we cannot keep those right under our nose, how can we keep anyone else?

So we cannot tell ourselves that we are only responsible for ourselves, but neither can we tell ourselves that we are not responsible for ourselves because others are responsible for us. Though its excesses are rightly and regularly pilloried by those of a more progressive and socialist sensibility, conservative American Protestants did not invent the idea of the Protestant work ethic. Something like it is found throughout Scripture, and Paul believed it essential to the flourishing of communities that faithfully bear the good news of the gospel. So while Paul admonishes his listeners to bear one another's burdens, he also has no patience for those who want to apply this to everyone but themselves.

For example, in a somewhat amusing and terrifying burst of rhetoric, Paul says that if you refuse to take responsibility to provide for your own household, you're not a Christian: "If anyone does not provide for his own, and especially for those of his household, he has denied the faith and is worse than an unbeliever" (1 Tim 5:8). Ask Jesus into your heart, receive holy communion every week of your life, serve the poor and powerless, believe with every fiber of your being, but if you don't responsibly provide for you and yours, you don't know Jesus.

More measured but no less serious are his remarks in Galatians and 2 Thessalonians—two passages that uniquely embody Scripture's firm but kind attitude toward responsibility. In Galatians 6, Paul challenges us to bear the burdens of others while not shirking the responsibility to bear our own burdens as well:

> Bear one another's burdens, and thereby fulfill the law of Christ. For if anyone thinks he is something when he is nothing, he deceives himself. But each one must examine his own work, and then he will have reason for boasting in regard to himself alone, and not in regard to another. For each one will bear his own load. (Gal 6:2–5)

In 2 Thessalonians, Paul is very critical of undisciplined, irresponsible people who expect others to be responsible for them. Paul asserts that he teaches and practices the exact opposite—that instead of expecting others to be responsible for his burdens, he takes both his burdens and the burdens of others upon himself to unburden others:

> Now we command you, brethren, in the name of our Lord Jesus Christ, that you keep away from every brother who leads an unruly life and not according to the tradition which you received from us. For you yourselves know how you ought to follow our example, because we did not act in an undisciplined manner among you, nor did we eat anyone's bread without paying for it, but with labor and hardship we kept working night and day so that we would not be a burden to any of you; not because we do not have the right to this, but in order to offer ourselves as a model for you, so that you would follow our example. For even when we were with you, we used to give you this order: if anyone is not willing to work, then he is not to eat, either. For we hear that some among you are leading an undisciplined life, doing no work at all, but acting like busybodies. Now such persons we command and exhort in the Lord Jesus Christ to work in quiet fashion and eat their own bread. But as for you, brethren, do not grow weary of doing good. If anyone does not obey our instruction in this letter, take special note of that person and do not associate with him, so that he will be put to shame. Yet do not regard him as an enemy, but admonish him as a brother. (2 Thess 3:6–15)

We must make ourselves responsible for others, but we must not make others responsible for us. To be a Christian is to be responsible for the sins and struggles of all—an all that primarily takes the form of one's self, one's household, one's church, one's neighbor, and whoever else one might come across, a responsibility made bearable because God in Christ has gladly taken responsibility for us.

"GOD, SMITE GEORGE BUSH"

Shortly after 9/11, and America's subsequent declaration of war upon Iraq, a group of activist students gathered for prayer. The prayer was convened by Will Willimon, dean of the chapel at Duke, and a plainspoken pacifist. He started things off with a good old-fashioned imprecatory prayer: "God, smite George Bush." This prayer opened the floodgates, and the imprecatory prayers proceeded to rain down from the students' mouths.

Last up in the prayer circle was professor Stanley Hauerwas, a god among mortals on campus, and *the* plainspoken pacifist. It would be tough to find someone more critical of America's thirst for war. (Hauerwas has gone so far as to call it a liturgical act for Americans.) Everyone in the circle anxiously awaited his imprecatory finale. They would be disappointed.

"Lord, be with George Bush. He has got to be at a difficult place in his life this morning. Lord, please forgive us for leading this good man into doing some sad things because of our lust to have somebody protect us and make security for us.... Forgive us for leading George Bush into this."[141]

If we can learn to gather as a convocation of the guilty but forgiven instead of the affronted and accusatory, to be a people who are slow to place blame and quick to take responsibility, perhaps the joyful and just song of Christianity will rise above the clash of victimocracies. Tired of unjust silence and aggrieved noise, perhaps we will join in the melody of the kingdom.

6

Righteousness Porn
So You Think You're a Prophet?

SO YOU THINK YOU'RE a prophet—speaking truth to power, punching up, telling it how it is, confounding the arrogant, scattering the proud, humbling the mighty? And maybe you are, but maybe you are not. False prophets abound, and the falsest are those convinced they are true. So if you were more false prophet than prophet, how would you know?

I used to think I was a prophet—not the future and fortune-telling kind, but the truth-telling kind. As a recovering fundamentalist evangelical, I relished sniping fundamentalist buffoons from my lofty theological perch. It was easy, fun, righteous. My rhetoric was fierce, my condescension severe, but they were dumb and demented and deserving. But I was no prophet.

I'm a firm believer everybody needs somebody who can tell them to shut the hell up, especially putative prophets. I can take no particular credit for having a number of such people in my life for I did my best to get rid of them, but God has seen fit to punish them by binding them to me. I learned I was not a prophet when, on the heels of posting a withering tweet related to the imbecility of rapturous fundamentalist evangelical support for a certain presidential candidate, one of my moral chaperones pointed out I had a rather insufferable tendency to confess other people's sins. And that, on a related note, I might consider shutting the hell up. I considered telling him to do the same, but, as he was an elder at my church, this seemed unwise, so I sat with it.

How dare he question my prophetic *bona fides*? Couldn't he see I was speaking truth to power? But as it turns out, imagining the prophetic task as simply "speaking truth to power" is just true enough to get one into trouble (and not "good" trouble), and much of what passes nowadays as "prophetic" is not speaking truth to power but speaking to your constituency about another constituency's problems, which is to say, being a twerp. So once again, maybe you are a prophet, but maybe you are not. How do you know?

THE PROPHETIC IMAGINATION

Walter Brueggemann knows prophets, and his book *The Prophetic Imagination* is a gem, mined from a thorough, patient excavation of the role of the prophet in Israel's history. According to him, the prophet's primary vocation is to keep alive the ministry of imagination, defined more specifically as a commitment to challenge "the way it is" with "the way God says it is," and all this rooted most specifically in the formation of an alternative community (Israel and church) that stubbornly and joyfully lives out God's order in defiance of the status quo.[142] This means prophets must both criticize and energize, must dismantle the oppression that bureaucrats call order and electrify us with the promise of God's joyfully just and impending future.[143]

Our greatest strengths are our greatest weaknesses, so it should come as little surprise prophets are a rare breed in the conservative mainland, for the spirit of conservativism is that of *conserving* the status quo. Not only is this not all bad, but it can be a great good. There are many things worth conserving. Change is not always better. History is not an inevitable march toward moral progress. Thank God for conservatives! The prophetic paucity of conservatives is not all bad, but it's not all good either because many things are not worth conserving.

An early document from the liberation theology camp in Puebla noted that while the cry of the oppressed was once muted it is now "loud and clear, increasing in volume and intensity, and at times full of menace."[144] And who typically doesn't like voices full of menace? Conservatives. Menace, after all, is not well suited to the conservation of the status quo.

But if we are to assign blame for the rising menace within historically oppressed groups and those claiming to advocate for them, that blame (as noted previously) must first be assigned to the Christ who barked woes upon the rich and ruling, and blessedness upon the poor and pitiful. In doing so, Christ is well situated within the prophetic tradition of Israel, assuming the mantle of Israel's first prophet, Moses: "The Lord makes a distinction between Egypt and Israel" (Exod 11:7).

Perhaps you have heard God doesn't take sides, but you didn't hear it from God. When the Hebrews cry out to God against Egypt and for liberation, God is a vicious partisan—not a neutral umpire. God does distinguish between Egypt and Israel; God does not flinch from taking Israel's side. And Moses the first Israelite prophet is Yahweh's avatar, standing with Israel and against Egypt, speaking with a voice full of menace. And who does like voices full of menace? Progressives. The spirit of conservativism is conserving the status quo, but the spirit of progressivism is *critiquing* the status quo, which means prophets (or at least alleged ones) proliferate in more progressive habitats. It's in the air, the water, the *zeitgeist*. And thank God for progressives!

RIGHTEOUSNESS PORN

But again, our greatest strengths are our greatest weaknesses, and the progressive appetite for critique easily mutates into "critiquiness," a phenomenon best described by Rita Felski as "an unmistakable blend of suspicion, self-confidence, and indignation."[145] And Felski's "critiquiness" fits snugly beside Sarah Silverman's "righteousness porn," and righteousness porn posing as prophecy is a perennial progressive problem, perhaps especially so right now.

So we have unprophetic conservatives and pseudo-prophetic progressive scolds aplenty but few genuine prophets because in addition to speaking truth to power, prophets in the biblical tradition practice "total identification." Speaking specifically of Isaiah but applicable to the biblical prophetic tradition at large, John Oswalt observes that prophets often spoke against Israel, but this *against* was situated within a deeper posture of *with* and *for* Israel:

> None can stand off in self-righteousness and say that his or her sinfulness is relatively less significant than someone else's. Neither is the prophet separating himself from the condition of his people. This capacity for total identification, with God on the one hand and the people on the other, is one characteristic of the Hebrew prophets. They are not disembodied voices, chirping . . .[146]

Prophets don't chirp at *them*; prophets confess for *us*.

Brueggemann affirms Oswalt's insight, making it plain the prophetic vocation requires total identification with the accused or else it is merely righteousness porn.

> Prophetic imagination requires more than the old liberal confrontation if the point is not posturing but effecting change in social perspective and social policy.[147]
> The prophet does not scold or reprimand.[148]
> If we are to understand prophetic criticism, we must see that its characteristic idiom is anguish and not anger.[149]
> Prophetic ministry does not consist of spectacular acts of social crusading or of abrasive measures of indignation.[150]
> Jeremiah can feel empathy for the royal folk. He yearns for the peace as much as they do. . . . The tear in the heart of Jeremiah is unspeakable. He does not gloat or rejoice. He would rather this king could rescue royal Judah—but it is very late.[151]

It all culminates in the crucifixion, the ultimate act of prophetic criticism because it is also the ultimate act of total identification:

> Therefore we say that the ultimate criticism is that God embraces the death that God's people must die. The criticism consists not in standing over against but in standing with; the ultimate criticism is not one of triumphant indignation but one of the passion and compassion that completely and irresistibly undermine the world of competence and competition.[152]

Brueggemann closes by reminding us that true prophecy is constituted by the total identification of the crucifixion, and if it is not so constituted then it's only antagonistic chirping: "Without the cross, prophetic imagination will likely be as strident and as destructive as that which it criticizes. The cross is the assurance that effective prophetic criticism is done not by an outsider but always by one who must embrace the grief, enter into the death, and know the pain of the criticized one."[153]

And this refusal to totally identify with the criticized and accused is the scarlet letter marking out chirping, pseudo-prophetic scolds. It is a scarlet letter I have borne before and still bear often because contempt for your own people is, I'm embarrassed to say, an occupational hazard for pastors and Christian "thought leaders" in particular. Hauerwas said it, so we know it's true:

> What I fear oftentimes is a temptation of those of us who are quite critical of the contemporary church is we can be lured into

contempt against the people that now make up the church. And contempt is a vice that invites you to feel superior to the people that you are serving. And I think the cynicism that oftentimes grips the lives of people in the ministry today that borders on contempt, is one of the things that we have to strongly resist.[154]

Beware critics who are contemptuous of their subject.

And if contempt for your people is enticing, contempt for *them* is outright bliss, which brings me back to my (and perhaps your) insufferable tendency to confess other people's sins.

SPECKS AND LOGS

It is impossible for a Christian to justify confessing the sins of others more than one's own, so we evade having to justify it by telling ourselves we're *not* doing it when we obviously *are*. Jesus' famous teaching on judgment seems applicable, and we know it well: "Why do you look at the speck that is in your brother's eye, but do not notice the log that is in your own eye?" (Matt 7:3).

As has been duly noted in more recent biblical scholarship, most of the *yous* in Scripture are plural, meaning Jesus' general condemnation of confessing the sins of others is not just individual but group, tribal, communal counsel. And while for the reasons outlined above the progressive zeitgeist tends to produce more pseudo-prophetic scolds than its conservative counterpart, Jesus' command to exercise extreme caution when confessing the sins of others is disobeyed with impunity by both progressives and conservatives, especially in relation to each other.

I should add such disobedience is also completely understandable and natural because part of what makes progressives progressive is they are not conservative, just as part of what makes conservatives conservative is they are not progressive. So if your sensibilities are more conservative, and you (broadly speaking) cherish the stability of the status quo, you are likely to feel a moral imperative to stand against those who delight in criticizing the status quo, and vice versa. But Jesus questions the morality of your allegedly moral imperative. No, it's probably not your job to criticize them.

Most of us have a habit of most concerning ourselves with what should least concern us. Take the odd kerfuffle that has recently unfolded in the Southern Baptist Convention over critical race theory. A lot of Southern Baptists apparently feel a moral imperative to combat it, but it is hard to think of a group less susceptible to the excesses of CRT than Southern Baptists. Surely the Amish are more susceptible to the excesses of transhumanist technology than the SBC is to CRT. Conversely, Christian nationalism is about as fashionable among progressive ideologues as a Confederate flag, but they seem genuinely unable to avoid chronically fretting about it ("You know what this podcast needs? More cowbell.").[155] So there are tribes that struggle with the excesses of critical theories, and tribes that struggle with the temptation of Christian nationalism, and both tribes are obsessed with fixing *them* instead of them*selves*.

But if we don't criticize them, who will? This will be tough to hear, but God, I am told, has his ways, and they do not require you nearly as much as you think. God can, does, and will raise up *bona fide* prophets in their midst who will thunder forth with prophetic menace, but do so situated within a posture of total identification that you cannot muster. Obviously, we do not believe it and so instead stay locked in childish, sinful filibuster, fixated on their specks instead of our logs.

Gutierrez says oppressed groups must embrace the role of the protagonist in their own stories, meaning they must embrace their agency instead of delegating the role of protagonist to more privileged groups who will "protagonize" on their behalf: "The most important part will have to be played by persons who themselves belong to these groups, despite the difficulties in the way of their doing so. It is not possible for others simply to stand up and effectively play the part of the protagonist."[156]

Esau McCaulley has said something similar, describing the way black theologians are often sandwiched between white progressives and white evangelicals bickering about black theology and racial justice, and rarely allowed to speak for themselves as the white progressives and evangelicals protagonize away for them (and *instead of* them).[157] Likewise, it is unwise to assign yourself the primary role of lead antagonist in someone else's story.

Another way we avoid acknowledging the grossness of obsessively confessing others' sins is by pretending we are a part of a tribe we are not. This action sounds malicious but is usually unintentional—less a matter of a wolf in sheep's clothing and more a matter of a white wolf imagining itself a sheep because it is white. We've now entered the territory of what we might, affectionately (and in David Attenborough's dignified, hushed voice), call the white progressive inquisitor. Wendell Berry explains the inquisitor's mission well:

> A great many white liberals have surpassed their own sinlessness to take upon themselves the race prejudice, racism, and racial violence of their ancestors, or of other people's ancestors. Because there is thus no limit to the number of ancestors, and no limit to the number of supposable ancestral sins, the burden of guilt to be borne by these otherwise guiltless white people is exceedingly great and painful to bear. This suffering they offer to their black allies as expiation or amends for racist abuses going back to the beginning of slavery. Any attempt at score-settling, however possible it may be, can thus be no small thing, nothing so ordinarily human as friendship or neighborliness or help in solving a local problem. No. What is called for is something public, large, symbolic, and monumental.[158]

And as mentioned above, I was once an inquisitor or something like it. Wanting to repent of white nationalism and racism on behalf of all white people, wanting to declare complicity in colossal injustices, the white progressive inquisitor genuinely believes he is confessing his sins, and it might even look like confession at a distance, but upon closer inspection it's often just more well-intentioned righteousness porn caused by the thirst for the immediate deed: white progressives confessing the purported sins of white conservatives. And as many have pointed out, we would do well to more carefully consider the appropriateness of white *appropriation* of black anger. For when white progressives attempt to appropriate and express black anger, one cannot help but sense it is often something besides black anger that is expressed.

Along these lines, while Martin Luther King Jr.'s white moderate critique must haunt us, we must also guard against employing it too metaphorically. In context, King was critiquing white people who were sympathetic (or at least not hostile) to the civil rights cause but felt black people should gently and patiently work towards and hope for legal equality instead of aggressively fighting for it. King's "white moderate" was a nice white person who was unwilling to fight for black civil rights.

But in current white progressive race rhetoric, a white moderate has become anyone who thinks anti-racist activism is not the truth, the whole truth, and nothing but the truth about race. It is wielded as a searing but vague accusation against everyone who is not as progressive as defined by progressive activists on race. One is often left with the rather uncomfortable impression that many white progressive inquisitors must think King himself a white moderate by their standards.

IF ALL YOU'RE DOING IS CASTING STONES . . .

So confessing the sins of others, under whatever auspices, is not prophetic but gross, tacky, and sinful. We rightly reprimand our children when they habitually tattle but applaud ourselves and our tribe when we do so under the guise of prophetic truth-telling. It's probably also important to note it doesn't work.

Commenting on sincere but ineffective forms of activism and agreeing more than a little with Dostoyevsky about the "thirst for the immediate deed," Barack Obama spoke plainly to a group of aspiring leaders in Chicago: "There's this sense sometimes of the way of me making changes is to be as judgmental as possible about other people, and that's enough. . . . But that's not activism. That's not bringing about change. If all you're doing is casting stones, you're probably not going to get that far."[159] Volf argues on similar lines:

> Today's critique, as a rule, offers no positive alternative; its normativity is antinormative. Unlike the prophets of old, many theologians today . . . shy away from offering a positive vision in whose service they undertake their critique. . . . In the absence of a positive vision, critiques easily devolve into mere griping, knocking things down. Unmasking gives the impression of intellectual profundity, and griping offers the cheap thrill of understated self-righteousness. Both get old quickly and accomplish little. . . . To change the world, we need an "I have a dream" speech, not an "I have a complaint" speech.[160]

And David Burrell years ago described the difference between a constructive response and an ideological reaction: "the first, by definition, alters the patterns of our own lives, while the second rails against 'them.'"[161]

Whilst practicing that most sacred and ancient Christian discipline of shutting the hell up recommended by one of my elders, I took a trip down the memory lane of my Twitter/X posts over that past year. This proved a painful audit. I did have an insufferable tendency to confess other people's sins, and while it was cathartic for me, it was helpful for nobody. To choose one example among many, it was clear upon reflection that my preferred tactic of condescension and accusation was not helping the white evangelicals under my care move toward a place a deeper racial awareness, empathy, humility, and justice. I had assumed an adversarial and contemptuous posture toward them, and they intuited it on a gut level.

I've since learned that if you want to facilitate a truer racial reckoning among conservative white Christians, encourage them to sit at the feet of black pastors and mute the shrill chirping of white progressive scolds. Why? Because black preachers tend to be motivated by organic righteous indignation, while white progressive scolds seem mostly motivated by volcanic contempt. You know it when you hear it—the bass of righteous indignation drowned out by an overload of contemptuous treble in the mix.

In many ways the father of black liberation theology in America, James Cone, is a prophet. His *The Cross and the Lynching Tree* is a fierce text, full of menace, but there is nothing pornographic in the righteousness on display within. Cone has somehow embraced the posture of an advocate fighting for us instead of an antagonist scolding them, and even when he stands menacingly against various forms of white supremacy, it is clear this stand *against* is but an expression of a more determinative stand *with* and *for*. The book closes with one of the most prophetic paragraphs one will find:

> Whites may be bad brothers and sisters, murderers of their own black kin, but they are *still* our sisters and brothers. We are bound together in America by faith and tragedy. All the hatred we have expressed toward one another cannot destroy the profound mutual love and solidarity that flow deeply between us. . . . No two people in America have had more violent and loving encounters than black and white people. . . . No gulf between blacks and whites is too great to overcome, for our beauty is more enduring than our brutality. What God joined together, no one can tear apart.[162]

This is what a prophet sounds like. Do you think you're a prophet?

7

Conservative and Progressive
A Better Story Together

I WAS DESTINED TO be conservative.

My father was raised rigidly Church of Christ, my mother Methodist, so compromise dictated I would be raised Southern Baptist. No upbringing is perfect, but mine was good. I was taught to love the Bible, tell people about Jesus, respect authority, and take responsibility for my actions. Conservatives do not have a monopoly on these goods, but they are particularly good at imparting them to their children.

But my conservative destiny was thwarted when I fell in love with an Episcopal girl. This says little considering everyone to the left of Billy Graham is progressive to a Southern Baptist boy, but I found my wife-to-be and her Episcopalian instincts baffling, maybe heretical. For these Episcopalians prayed odd and formal prayers, talked a lot about social justice, let women do some of the talking, and suggested authority needs challenging and not just respecting. But resistance was futile, and when that stout Port communion wine, dryer than dust, hit my palette, I knew I would never settle for conservative grape juice again.

I also went to college, where, as has been well-documented, conservatism goes to die, at least for a while. From here the story becomes embarrassingly predictable.

I was enlightened, emerging from the conservative cave in which I was raised and all other conservative Neanderthals still exist, and the most important thing about me was that I was not a conservative because conservatives are the worst. They are also dumb and racist. So it was settled: I would be a progressive. The Anne Lamott corpus pushed the John Piper collection out of view and into a dusty, haphazard stack behind another dusty, haphazard stack on the highest shelf. Freedom!

But can one have too much freedom?

While exploring the expanding theological, social, and moral universe opened up before me in my progressive conversion, I wondered. Because it felt good to be unshackled, but after a time I sensed unshackled easily becomes untethered, which is its own kind of shackle. Then Stanley Hauerwas staged an intervention.

"You don't get to make Christianity up."

I can't remember where I first encountered Hauerwas saying this, primarily because everything he says is saying this, but when I heard it, I knew it was true and my progressive days were numbered.

American's "best" theologian (at least so said *Time* magazine) was decidedly not a conservative. The scathing diatribes he has delivered against Christian nationalism and fundamentalist evangelicalism are the stuff of legend. And despite claims to the contrary, conservatives are just as prone to make Christianity up as their liberal and progressive nemeses, only instead of making Christianity up by subtracting from it (the standard liberal and progressive temptation), conservatives make Christianity up by adding to it. It usually takes the form of taking clearly nonessential, non-creedal beliefs about things like the nature of the inspiration of the Bible, the authority of males over females, and absolute and utter allegiance to the Christian Right, and smuggling them into orthodoxy. But making Christianity up by addition is still making Christianity up, so I wasn't going back to being a conservative.

Hauerwas was not a conservative but having garnered a well-deserved reputation as the sworn enemy of Protestant liberalism, neither was he a liberal. The differences between liberal and progressive Christianity can be opaque. Liberals are more bound to Enlightenment rationalism, trust more in "reason," and pride themselves in objectivity. In a word, they are very *modern*. Progressives have a more activist streak, think "reason" is often another form of oppression, and above all pride themselves in being allies of those on the bottom half of the intersectionality axis. In a few words, they are *modern but on the way to something like postmodern*.

Liberal Christianity is calm, cool, collected, mushy, and struggles finding the gas. Progressive Christianity is passionate, heated, aggressive, shrill, and struggles finding the brakes.

These differences are real, but liberal and progressive Christians share a common spirit, probably best described as an attraction to novelty. The liberal/progressive mind has an appetite for newness, which is why we all aspire to love anything as much as an old liberal hippie or young progressive urbanite loves talking about the new Greek restaurant in midtown. An appetite for newness is wonderful but can also make one overly accommodating to ideological fashion, and more than a little willing to make Christianity up by subtracting from it when and where it has become unfashionable. Of course, not all liberals or progressives do this, just as not all conservatives burn incense before tiny Buddha-like Donald Trump figurines after evening prayer, but it is an occupational hazard of the liberal/progressive mind.

I should also disclose that Hauerwas's intervention coincided with the birth of my first child, and while I was struggling devilishly with my faith at the time, I rather wanted my children to be Christians, and it became clear to me that liberals and progressives, for their many gifts, did not have the gift of passing on their faith to their children in great measure.

This is a fact and not an observation made with any glee. No matter how we slice the data, it is clear that those raised in more liberal and progressive expressions of Christianity are much more likely to walk away from Christianity than those raised in less liberal and progressive expressions of Christianity.[163] And for all the progressive crowing about people leaving the church, the most typical "leaving church" story is not that of the fundamentalist evangelical turned ex-vangelical but the slow, silent exodus of the children of liberals and progressives.

Charles Taylor observes that viewed historically, it's clear early modern forms of liberal Christianity were the antechamber to modern secularism and unbelief.[164] How could it be otherwise? Why bother being Deist or Unitarian when you can just be agnostic? There's not enough gravity to keep you in orbit. So while it would be overly simplistic to say I am not a liberal or progressive Christian because I'd like my children to be Christian, it is not entirely untrue. Mostly, though, I just didn't want to make Christianity up; or better, I wanted to make sure I was making it up as little as possible.

Thanks to Anne Lamott, I could not be a conservative. Thanks to Stanley Hauerwas, I could not be a liberal or progressive. Thanks to Martin

Luther King Jr., I could not be a moderate. What could I be? What are you if you're too conservative to be a progressive, but too progressive to be a conservative, but too privileged to let yourself get away with being a moderate?[165]

LEFT OR RIGHT OR UP?

Fear not—no rope-a-dope ode to the virtues of centrism is forthcoming. Moderate Christianity has less gravitas than a dust mote wandering the Milky Way. Rather, what I found and find myself increasingly drawn to is not a set conservative or moderate or progressive identity, but is more like a tactic, a posture, an attitude. James C. Scott says something like what I'm trying to say when he makes the case for what he calls "the anarchist squint."[166]

Full-on anarchism is for children and professors so privileged and protected in their tenured towers they're free to tout the virtues of anarchism knowing full well they'll never face the consequences of actual anarchism. Not a set, comprehensive anarchist identity, the anarchist squint describes a tactic where one makes a habit of looking at the world from an anarchist angle, an angle typically at odds with those trying to tell us the big, official stories about the way things are.

Christopher Watkin is on to something similar when he describes the Bible's tendency to "diagonalize" things we mistake as binary choices. For example, does God will things because they are good, or are things good because God willed them? Is there a law of goodness external to God but by which God must abide (in which case the law of goodness and not God would appear to be God), or does God arbitrarily define the good by God's actions (in which case the word *good* has lost all meaning)? Neither. Rather, God's only obligation is to be fully free to be fully himself, and because God in himself is infinitely good, goodness is neither determined by a law external to God nor arbitrarily defined by God.

And Scripture is filled with this kind of diagnolizing of what we presume to be binary choices: "To diagonalize a choice in this way is to refuse the two (or more) alternatives it offers and elaborate a position that is neither reducible nor utterly unrelated to them."[167]

As I have tried to describe it, playing the justice + friendship tension is a practice similar to the anarchist squint, biblical diagonalizing, Barthian dialectics, Hegelian *aufhenbung*, Christo-verticality. Rejecting settled identities on the flat horizon of left to right, we settle upon an us-for-them commitment to stay unsettled in our ideological identities so we can stay critically fair and friendly to the varied gifts that come to us from all over. Instead of only looking right and left in suspicion, we look up and down with curiosity. We long to be pulled into the elevation of the kingdom so we are not pulled apart by the either/or tug-of-war. We embody a theory that is friendly and not just critical because while we might have enemies, we dare not *need* them.

According to novelist Gail Godwin, there are two kinds of people—not conservative or progressive, but fluid or congealed:

> One kind you can tell just by looking at them at what point they congealed into their final selves. It might be a very nice self, but you know you can expect no more surprises from them. Whereas the other keeps moving, changing . . . That doesn't mean they're unstable. Ah, no, far from it. They are fluid. They keep moving forward . . . and the motion of it keeps them young. In my opinion, they are the only people who are still alive. You must be constantly on your guard . . . against congealing.[168]

Once you allow the ideological concrete to set around your feet, you become numbingly boring, and be it a conservative or progressive boring, we can expect no more surprises from you.

Our other option is not instability, but fluidity. We are stable, but nimble. We are not conservative *or* progressive because we are conservative *and* progressive.

ONCE UPON A TIME . . .

Here are two stories. You will probably like one of them.

> Once upon a time, the vast majority of human persons suffered in societies and social institutions that were unjust, unhealthy, repressive, and oppressive. These traditional societies were reprehensible because of their deep-rooted inequality, exploitation, and irrational traditionalism. . . . But the noble aspiration for autonomy, equality, and prosperity struggled mightily against the forces of misery and oppression, and eventually succeeded in establishing modern, liberal, democratic, capitalist, welfare societies. While modern social conditions hold the potential to maximize the individual freedom and pleasure of all, there is much work to be done to dismantle the powerful vestiges of inequality, exploitation, and

repression. This struggle for the good society in which individuals are equal and free to pursue their self-defined happiness is the one mission truly worth dedicating one's life to achieving.[169]

Once upon a time, America was a shining beacon. Then liberals came along and erected an enormous federal bureaucracy that handcuffed the invisible hand of the free market. They subverted our traditional American values and opposed God and faith at every step of the way. . . . Instead of adhering to traditional American values of family, fidelity, and personal responsibility, they preached promiscuity. . . . Instead of projecting strength to those who would do evil around the world, they cut military budgets, disrespected our soldiers in uniform, burned our flag. . . . Then Americans decided to take their country back from those who sought to undermine it.[170]

The first story, composed by sociologist Christian Smith, is what we might call "The Progressive Story." Liberation is the key concept, the electricity bringing the story to life. The past is bleak, a wasteland of oppression. An increasingly inclusive, equitable, and just future is our mission.

"For People, For a Change"
"Building a Bridge to the 21st Century"
"Change We Can Believe In"
"Forward"

These are the recent campaign slogans for Democratic presidential candidates, and they all put the accent *forward*, on progress. Past = bad and unjust. Future = good and just. This is the story progressives tell about the world. It makes sense to them, and it makes sense of them. They are drawn by this story's irresistible gravity.

The second story, composed by clinical psychologist Drew Westen, is what we might call "The Conservative Story." Fidelity is the key concept, the fire that fuels conservatism. The past, while imperfect, was good. Our mission is conserving the order, heritage, and values that make us *us*.

"Make America Great Again"

Conservatives put the accent *back* on conservation. Past = good and faithful. Future = bad and unfaithful. This is the story conservatives tell about the world because it makes sense to and of them.

Almost everybody likes one of these stories; almost nobody likes both. They are stories in conflict. Is the past mostly bad or mostly good? Is our mission liberation or conservation? Inclusion at all costs or fidelity at all costs? Yet while this presents itself as a conflict, it's a tension waiting to be played. Like the apparent clash between justice and friendship, this is not a duel but a duet, an opportunity to do the anarchist squint, diagonalize, go vertical, and stay fluid instead of congealed. One of the New Testament's most consequential stories is the story of the early Christians living this conservative/progressive tension instead of rejecting it as an irreconcilable conflict.

A THEOLOGY OF FORESKINS

The apostle Paul has been traveling the ancient world proclaiming the good news about Jesus the Messiah, and to mostly everyone's surprise, Jews are mostly rejecting the crucified Jewish messiah, whereas gentiles are receiving him in great number. Modern Christian gentiles are incapable of feeling the full force of the resulting dilemma.

To be sure, Israel's history was filled with hints something like this might happen. God told Abraham his election and resulting blessed family was to redound to the blessing of all the families of the earth. Prophets like Zechariah later declared an impending pilgrimage of the nations to Jerusalem (Zech 2:11, 8:22). Isaiah delivered God's summons unto salvation that extends to the ends of the earth (Isa 45:22). Perhaps we should say a dominant plotline in Israel's story is the increasing conviction that even non-Jewish people will come to worship Israel's God.

But the important proviso in this inclusivist strand of Jewish theology was that while gentiles could be accepted by the Jewish God, they would surely need to become Jewish first. Becoming Jewish meant following the Law of Moses, with its many moral, ceremonial, and dietary laws, and most importantly, it meant the gentile foreskins had to go because not even Israel's gracious God could accept an uncircumcised gentile. They can join us, but only if they become us.

These are the terms, and everybody knows they are iron-clad. But then something happens.

Paul has strange, unsettling experiences. Out there in the wilds of the sinful, pagan world, blasphemy is occurring at his hands, but beyond his control. Gentiles are receiving the gospel of Israel's Messiah and God, and God is receiving these gentiles in full even though they have not become Jewish yet. Bacon on their breath and foreskins firmly in place, they are nevertheless recipients of the outpouring of the Holy Spirit. More troubling still, Peter, the other most important Christian on the face of the planet at the time, has experienced similar. What to make of it? Are Paul and Peter committing blasphemy? Is God? Everyone convenes in Jerusalem in Acts 15 to sort it out.

The conservative Jewish Christians drive up in a stampede of F-150s, four homeschooled children shoulder-to-shoulder in the second row, Matthew's Gospel in hand. They admire Peter tremendously, and begrudgingly respect Paul, but sense both are straying from biblical authority. They want to impose a more gospel-centered (according to them) approach to the gentile brouhaha. Because although they're delighted the gentiles have come around to worshipping the one true God, the one true God gave the Law and commanded its keeping, which forbids the keeping of foreskins. So the church dare not neglect conserving the faith passed down in the name of progress.

The progressive Jewish Christians drive up in a parade of Subarus, rescue pets riding shotgun, Luke's Gospel at the ready. They appreciate their Jewish heritage, but they're also embarrassed by large parts of it. The bigotry has to go. No more demanding that converts take a stone blade to their genitals. Trust the inclusive, liberating experience and stop cowering before antiquated beliefs and laws. Jettison the old, embrace the new, pass the bacon.

"The apostles and the elders came together to look into this matter. After there had been much debate . . ." (Acts 15:6–7a).

One wishes the details of this "much debate" had been better documented, and no doubt the standard conservative accusations of heresy were leveled against the progressives, just as the standard progressive accusations of bigotry were leveled against the conservatives. But, thanks be to God, at least a couple of firm but friendly minds in the room discerned this was an occasion for collaboration, not an opportunity for battle.

Peter goes first. It might seem odd to suggest the first pope was progressive, but a good case could be made that given what he did in relation to the moment he inhabited, Peter was one of the most progressive thinkers in human history. And at a certain point in this fiercest of early Christian debates, he stands and makes an unashamedly experience-centered argument.

Everybody in the room experienced God's choosing of Peter to take the gospel to the gentiles. Peter has experienced God giving the Spirit to the gentiles *as* gentiles and not gentiles-turned-Jews. All of them have experienced their inability to bear the full yoke of the Law. All of them should embrace these experiences as a new revelation of God's will. And while Peter certainly knew and cherished the Hebrew Scriptures, he does not reach for them here but instead leans heavily and comfortably upon what he takes to be the undeniable revelation emerging from these shared experiences.

James goes next. History will come to give Peter a certain superiority to James, but James does not seem to see it that way, and upon reading Acts 15 one senses James carries more weight in the room. He speaks last and definitively: "Brethren, listen to me."

It's quickly clear that while James respects Peter and Peter's experience, his mind does not work the same way as Peter's. Their theological processes are not in complete alignment. They put the accent in different places. Their rational and emotional instincts differ. So whereas Peter's reflexes cause him to reach forward exploring this new experience, James' reflexes cause him to reach backward guarding the tradition. Commenting upon Simon Peter's experience-centered argument, James immediately reaches for his Hebrew Bible: "Simeon has related how God first concerned Himself about taking from among the Gentiles a people for His name. *With this the words of the Prophets agree,* just as it is written . . ." (Acts 15:14–15).

James arrives at the same place as Peter, but he must travel a different road. Good for Peter and his experience, but what do the Scriptures say? His mind is more conservative. He's open to progress but will not sacrifice fidelity. Happily, he, with Peter's help, discerns that in this instance fidelity need not be sacrificed at the altar of progress, nor progress at the altar of fidelity. What could and should have been the first volley in the infernal and eternal holy war between conservatives and progressives instead became an occasion for a collaboration that manifested the kingdom come in a way never before or since seen. The gentiles, *as gentiles,* are in. How do we know? Spirit and Scripture have spoken, not in narrow unison, but in layered harmony.

Faced with a tension between fidelity and progress, Peter and James made gospel music by playing the tension and allowing God to pull them up into something that was both faithful and new. They would embrace the surprising work of the Spirit, but they would not make Christianity up.

A BETTER STORY TOGETHER

We cannot force a formalized procedure out of Acts 15, but we can constantly receive it as a reminder the conservative/progressive tension should be cherished, not abolished or merely tolerated. Add to this Paul's assertion in 1 Corinthians 12 that God gives different manifestations of the Spirit to different people for the common good and in order that we might all need each other, and it's no stretch to conclude that God desires there be both conservatives and progressives.[171] This conclusion is made indisputable by the simple fact that a world full of conservatives or progressives would be hell.

And this is even more so I and not the Lord speaking, but it seems that God desiring conservatives and progressives further implies that God desires that conservatives know how and when to be progressive, and that progressives know how and when to be conservative, which might be another way of saying God desires that everybody, in their own way, be conservative *and* progressive.

Much is true, good, and beautiful in the progressive story. The judgment of the unjust and liberation of the oppressed is a story Scripture tells from cover to cover. And yet while parts of the story are true, the story as the whole story is a lie because Scripture refuses to let anybody comfortably settle into the role of critic, or neatly divide humanity up into pure victims and pure oppressors, pure poverty and pure privilege. And as much as many progressives hate the conservative story, staying in a humble and healthy conversation with it ensures that the progressive story does not devolve into an unworthy cover of itself—"The Critical Nightmare."

Much is true, good, and beautiful in the conservative story. Everything that calls itself progress has not been progress. Victimocracy cannot save the world. We must conserve our families and faith from the corrosion wrought by secularism. And yet while parts of the story are true, the story as the whole story is a lie because the "prosperity" of our families and country cannot be our ultimate concern because they are not God's ultimate concern. And as much as conservatives hate the progressive story, a friendly dialogue with it ensures that the conservative story does not mutate into the heresy also known as "The American Dream"—a heresy prevalent in varied forms in all empires, from the beginning of time.

Conservatives and progressives tell a better story together than they tell apart.

AN UNWITTING CONSPIRACY OF FOES

But there is a long-standing conspiracy afoot to suppress this co-authorship, especially dangerous because it is an unwitting conspiracy of foes. Here's how it works. True believers on the right and left unwittingly conspire to make healthy, humble, and critically friendly dialogue impossible by mistaking a collaborative tension for a holy war where we must pursue victory at all costs. And once we convince ourselves we're in a victory-at-all-costs holy war, truth and communion are the casualties of that war.

Sergei Bulgakov knew holy war. The son of a Russian Orthodox priest, he entered seminary and promptly lost his faith because his professors could not answer his questions. He next studied law, making a name for himself as a bright, young Marxist. But staying every bit as critical of Marxism as Marxism was of most everything else, he migrated toward something like Christian socialism, having been drawn back into the orbit of faith. He was a rebel at heart but felt increasingly uneasy about the irresponsible self-righteousness he discerned in revolutionary Russian leftists.

Then his four-year-old son died. He had a profound experience at the funeral that, it seems, solidified his faith. Around ten years later, he became a priest. Prodigal turned atheist Marxist turned Christian socialist turned Orthodox priest.

He lost his teaching post in the aftermath of the Bolshevik Revolution and was kicked out of Russia shortly thereafter. He died in Paris, to his great grief. In addition to asking for as inexpensive and simple a funeral as possible, his only other request was that a handful of soil be taken from his son's grave in Russia and placed in his.

Having no vested interest in modern American holy wars, Bulgakov's political theology is especially relevant because of its irrelevance. He believed the Russian activist left erred in making a religious idol of social justice and revolution. He was especially critical of activist progressive Christians for capitulating to an arrogant historical amnesia wherein they date history's beginning with themselves. But he believed the Russian religious right erred in stubbornly holding to tradition and thus failing to understand how injustice inevitably insinuates itself into powerful institutions over time. He believed the progressive Christian left and traditional religious right were both merely playing the secular power game, only they were more dangerous and deluded than their secular counterparts because the most dangerous and deluded people are always the people sure God is on their side.

Bulgakov also saw that progressives and conservatives had an uncanny ability to draw out the worst in each other: "Socialist utopians . . . make of social revolution a religious idol. But on the opposite side, the people of the Church see this as sufficient ground for condemning the socialist utopianists and for washing their hands of any personal responsibility. There arises mutual estrangement, deafness, and a lack of understanding."[172]

Charles Taylor calls this phenomenon "mutually supportive opposition."[173] We see *their* errors and hypocrisies clearly, fixate on them, and this fixation makes us blind to their insights and gifts (which often rightfully point out our errors and hypocrisies) and far too sure of ourselves.

The debate over race in America is a sad example. As Anthony B. Bradley prophesied via tweet, progressives see conservative reticence to address race, and feel justified in claiming white racism is the cause of everything wrong in black communities. But race problems in America cannot be reduced to a single variable, and progressives relentlessly attempting to do so helps no one. Conservatives see this error, plain as day to everyone who isn't progressive, and "weaponize it in service to their own self-righteousness."[174] Nothing changes, except our increased certainty that *they* are the problem and *we* are the solution. We push each other into deeper lunacy and delusion.

Once again, spite makes us stupid—literally. More interesting still, spite makes smart people especially stupid.[175] Holy warriors don't care about being fair; they care about winning. Thus, the spite of holy warriors leads them to make arguments that are much dumber than they might otherwise be.

The paradoxical implication is that friendliness actually enables us to become more critical (not less), in the healthiest sense of the term. No longer locked in mortal combat because instead joined in a collaborative venture for the common good, I can relieve myself of the burden of defeating you, which frees both of us to be more honest about our strengths and weaknesses, our blessings and curses. Because criticism is at its finest when it's not rendered dumb by spite.

Sounding much like the apostle Paul, Bulgakov asks, "And where many are prone to see a spiritual confrontation, in which all guilt is found solely on one side, is this not a certain misunderstanding created by intellectual poverty and ill will but also by the presence of guilt on the other side as well?"[176] He ends with what is, I hope, a familiar suggestion: "Unceasing renewal is the law and condition of spiritual life, as well as of fidelity to living tradition."[177] In other words, Bulgakov calls for a fluid, ongoing alliance between the fire of revolution and the stability of fidelity.

Fast-forward from early twentieth-century Russian politics into the world of music and twenty-first-century organ-making, and Matthew Crawford offers a similar analysis. The major tension in the organ-making community is, apparently (like every community with a history) the tension between those who crave new challenges and those who find dignity in the old ways. I'll spare you the details, but Crawford reminds us that any healthy tradition must exist in "an ongoing dynamic of reverence and rebellion."[178] All reverence creates bureaucrats and a petrified tradition. All rebellion creates amateurs and the death of all traditions except death to all traditions, which is the dumbest of traditions.

Reverence is a prerequisite to holy rebellion. Rebellion keeps reverence reverent. We must bow our heads and raise our fists.

THE CENTER ~~MUST~~ WILL HOLD

A rift is opening—old but new. Tension is building deep beneath the ideological surface, and rather than ripping open in a singular bang, the rift slowly gapes. Because the conservative/progressive fault line is so long, stretching out across space and time, it manifests itself differently in different places. As mentioned prior, two of the more interesting emerging rifts are the intramural ones between classical liberals and progressive activists on the one hand, and classic conservatives and MAGA acolytes on the other. But before Christians imagine ourselves responsible for addressing those rifts, we must attend to those in the household of faith.

Recent years revealed the extent to which many conservative Christians were Christian nationalists: willing to sell their souls for a bowl of patriotic lentils, grossly overdetermined by their spite of liberals and progressives. But liberals and progressives fumbled a profound opportunity to facilitate repentance and restoration for their conservative brethren. It was understandable, but tragic.

Because they stood against Trump and stared aghast at the derangement of many conservative Christian defenders of him, progressives became far too morally sure of themselves. They assumed their opposition to Trump surely signaled their righteousness about most everything else, and they became cringingly comfortable with their self-righteousness. In this sense, Trump tested conservatives and progressives and moderates, and we all failed. He was not the president we needed, but it has become clear he was the president we deserved.

Our failure is a painful gift—an opportunity to remember God prefers the duet to the duel, an opportunity to remember the center must and will hold. But the center is not a set place, or a compromised politic, or a settled identity. The center is a commitment to get over ourselves so we can collaborate in our telling of the story of God in Christ because, by God's design, we tell it better together than we do apart.

8

Wendell Berry Would Like a Word
An Imaginary but Real Conversation Between an Old, White Farmer and a Young, Progressive Pastor on Trump, Whiteness, Friendship, Exaggeration, Anger, and the Unsettling of America

How to Have an Enemy is a good book. In the currently booming industry that is books written to scold white people and especially white Christians, it stands apart because its author, Melissa Florer-Bixler, is a sharp and sincere thinker. The book functions as a white paper on progressive Christianity's critique of nonprogressive Christianity, and more specifically, nonprogressive Christianity's failures to be a socially just expression of Christianity. She tries to be fair but pullls no punches. The book is full of menace.

In another life, it's a book I might have written. Not so long ago, I tracked closely with the major lines of the book's arguments. We must stop calling for unity and friendship and instead do justice and let the sky fall. We must call upon white Christians to repent of their whiteness and ally themselves with minorities, period and full-stop. We must choose sides, and to choose any side except that of the marginalized is to choose oppression. The greatest threat to Christianity is white evangelical Christianity.

I am, genuinely, glad the book was written, and it is a book well-written. But while reading it I was most struck that it was a book Wendell Berry had since rendered me incapable of writing.

I was drawn to Berry's work during the pandemic. For most of us, and especially for pastors, the pandemic was a reckoning in responsibility and a sorting out the shape of a little person's responsibility in a big world. Pastors are prone to the messiah complex, so when the pandemic hit, many of us felt a responsibility to take responsibility for the whole world and were quickly frustrated to find this was not a responsibility we could manage. Our pastoral frustration was compounded when, in those early days of the pandemic, we realized we were only capable of taking responsibility for ourselves, our families, and our immediate neighbors.

It was particularly humbling because most of us realized we were very good at talking about big ideas like justice, mission, and the Great Commission, but very bad at loving the small piece of creation that was actually ours to love. I am aware of no more sane perspective about the shape of a little person's responsibility in a big world than Wendell Berry, and his sanity helped me maintain some of mine during the insanity of the pandemic.

Reading the Berry corpus, most of which is quite old, I often wondered what he would say about the prevailing ideological holy wars. I drew the conclusions I thought appropriate, many of which shaped the early chapters of this book. But I worked under the assumption that I would have to make an educated guess as to what Berry would say given that he was, by his own admission, an old man, well into his eighties. I expected no more books from Wendell Berry.

But Abraham and Sarah expected no children, and when I learned Berry had indeed written another book, and a book about patriotism and prejudice at that, I laughed like Sarah and thanked God that Wendell Berry would like a word on the situation. So in the *aufhenbung* spirit of this book, I'd like to put Florer-Bixler and Berry's books in a conversation to see what kind of elevation their collaboration might yield.

Although Florer-Bixler is a young, white, female, urban progressive pastor and Berry is an old, white, male, rural farmer, it would be a mistake to think their viewpoints opposed. They agree on many things. They agree Jesus is Lord, white supremacy is America's founding sin, America continues to have a systemic race and justice problem, and Donald Trump was unfit to be president. Yet while not opposed, they do see things differently because they see different things. In the style of pointillism, let's talk specifics before stepping back to observe the big picture, and the most specific point of tension in our modern holy war is Donald Trump.

TRUMP

Florer-Bixler and Berry agree upon not voting for Trump but disagree on how we are to understand and what we are to do with those who did. The Sunday after the 2016 election, her church mourned: "We read psalms of lament and psalms of angry protest. We prayed for God's deliverance. But we did not pray for unity with Christians who supported the Republican candidate."[179] Given what she was seeing, this response made perfect theological sense and was felt with the force of a mandate. In many progressive minds, Donald Trump's victory was, categorically and without qualification, a victory of white supremacy; thus, Christians were theologically obligated to mourn and oppose it, for to do otherwise was to take the side of the oppressor.

This outlook was so clear that the question of whether there might be someone in her church that Sunday who had voted for Trump was irrelevant because to vote for Trump was to cast one's lot with injustice, and churches dare not become shelters of oppression in the name of unity: "I didn't consider if a Trump supporter might be in worship that morning in November, offended by the prayers and tears. It didn't matter. We needed a space to mourn."[180] In Florer-Bixler's mind, her church was constituted by a core "we" that did not include people who had voted for Donald Trump.

Though Berry does not say so explicitly, one senses he mourned the election of Trump as well, but he finds the conundrum of what to do with people who voted for him both more complicated and simple than Florer-Bixler does. As a rural person living among rural people, Berry is unable to see only white supremacy in Trump's election because his vision is complicated by the presence of those many supremacies progressives are reluctant to name: cosmopolitanism, elitism, classism.

Berry understands that while some people voted for Trump because they are explicit or implicit white supremacists, many, and probably most, did not. Berry understands that many rural people voted for Trump because they intuited that elitist progressives and liberals not only despise them but are religiously committed to both despising and not understanding them. Berry cannot let white supremacy be the only functioning political explanation at hand because he knows actual people who do not fit the explanation:

> I did not vote for Donald Trump. He affronts and endangers much to which my heart belongs. And I can go . . . so far as to say that I am sure some rural people are racist, sexist, and otherwise, by my standards, wrong. And I think it is likely that many of these people voted for Donald Trump. But at this point I would like to stop and think.
>
> My life has been long enough to permit me to know some people, some of them belonging to rural America, who were guilty of thinking some bad thoughts and doing some bad things. But as strongly as I have disliked some of these people . . . I do not think that any of them could be adequately or fairly characterized by listing their faults. The sorest of the growing pains of ignorance may be the discovery that most partly bad people are partly good, and that the best of us are no more than partly good.[181]

I know Pastor Florer-Bixler knows that, in her own words, "if we are to have enemies well, we first need to understand them."[182] And I believe that she believes she does, and I believe that she does have some understanding of some of those who voted for Trump, but I also believe it plain that Berry's understanding runs deeper.

So the matter of why people voted for Trump is complicated to Berry, but the matter of what to do with them is rather simple because there is no decision to be made—there is nowhere for him or them to go. Shunning people who voted for Trump was a pickiness unavailable to rural people:

> My family and I are not Trumpists, but there is no chance that we could live here and have to do only with people who voted as we did. That impossibility in fact reduces our interest in who voted for whom. Often we have no idea. Almost never do we try to find out. When on our visits to town we meet our neighbors face-to-face, it does not occur to us to question if they may be our political opponents. We are asking how they are, and how are their families, and did they get enough rain. Somebody tells a joke, and we laugh. . . . There is almost no talk of politics. Perhaps this is because we live more in the wide world than city people do. . . . In Port Royal, thanks mostly to its nature and circumstances, humanity remains a larger category than political allegiance.[183]

Shaking the dust off your feet in rebuke of your enemies as you depart their offending village is awkward when you cannot actually depart the offending village because it is your village. Berry is making an assertion bordering on an accusation: it is not rural people who are out of touch with the "real" world, but city people. And this is a severe and paradoxical limitation of the urbane point of view: "It is more limited than the rural point of view because it is much purer and more self-enclosed than the rural point of view."[184]

Rural people have not the luxury of waging something as theoretical as an ideological holy war because instead of abstract enemies, they have actual neighbors, and it is, generally speaking, impolite and unwise to wage war on a neighbor. After all, you might need to borrow some milk or have them watch your child. And so what Florer-Bixler does not consider, Berry cannot *not* consider. Waging our cultural conflicts as a holy war is a luxury unavailable to neighborly people.

WHITENESS

Related to what one sees when one sees a Trump voter, Florer-Bixler and Berry also see whiteness from different angles. Florer-Bixler calls a powerful ally to the stand in Willie Jennings, who sees whiteness as "a principality."[185] Whiteness names that demonic, colonizing spirit whereby the powerful enforce the conformity or destruction of the weak. We are possessed by whiteness when we seek to possess others. Summing up well the standard anti-racist view on whiteness, Florer-Bixler states that "whiteness is a corruption that takes hold of people, placing them under the power of a satanic order of systemic violence and degradation."[186]

Calling another powerful ally in W. E. B. Du Bois, Florer-Bixler suggests that poor white people voted for Trump even though doing so was (according to her) clearly against their self-interests because "the satanic power of belonging to whiteness" was a stronger draw than even their own self-interests.[187] A similar argument was made in a *Washington Post* piece in which the author, struggling with how so many minorities could have voted for Trump in 2020, used the concept of "multiracial whiteness" as an explanation.[188] The latter is a manifestation of the "becoming white" trope wherein systemic white racism lures all people, even minorities, toward whiteness, and any attraction poor people and minorities have toward anything nonprogressive is an understandable but sinful attraction to whiteness.[189]

There are many nuanced and important thoughts at work here. If you've delved into the anti-racist world, you know there is much sense to be made in it. But if you still have another foot in a world where anti-racism has some explaining to do, you might have some questions. You might question the wisdom of naming the satanic desire to oppress others "whiteness." You might question the charity of calling it racist and stupid but mainly racist when many people decline to cast their lot with a political party that's infused with an allegedly anti-racist ideology that casually calls whiteness demonic and them stupid for not simply agreeing.

When reading Florer-Bixler and Berry together, one quickly realizes that on both the general issue of racial justice and most of the specifics therein, both authors would think the other's view is too simplistic. We'll return to this idea, but as it pertains to whiteness, Florer-Bixler has no patience for the mannered assertion that because a lot of white people don't think of themselves as racist, we probably shouldn't casually equate whiteness with racism. Florer-Bixler finds that view simplistic because she believes she sees a whiteness conspiracy at work behind the curtain of well-mannered whiteness.

But while Florer-Bixler thinks she sees a conspiracy behind the curtain of well-mannered whiteness, Berry thinks he sees a conspiracy behind the curtain of anti-racism:

> As I write of the history that both divides and unites us, I am often tempted to wish it had been simpler and easier to understand. But the more I work to make it clear, the more complicated and obscure—and interesting—I find it to be. The racist argument has always been so simple as to need no comprehending. It simply divides the two categories, white people and black people, by a line theoretically straight, and opposes one category to the other. The actual history of the races . . . is complicated enough, questionable enough, and interesting enough to keep us reading and writing, asking and answering, talking to one another. . . . That is why it is distressing to see the antiracists resort to the same categories and draw essentially the same straight line as the racists.[190]

Is it too simple to say, as some do, that racism died, root and stem, with the victory of the civil rights movement? Absolutely. There is more behind the curtain. But is it not also too simple to keep drawing the same clumsy, straight line from white to racist, over and over, insisting that before any other lines might be drawn, we must all agree this is the only line that really matters? Is it possible that in addition to being an attempt at a complex and comprehensive accounting of systemic injustice and racism, conventional anti-racism also suffers the simple and foundational flaw of "drawing essentially the same straight line as the racists"?

Three's a crowd, but Jonathan Tran's *Asian Americans and the Spirit of Racial Capitalism* lifts the curtain higher yet, and his penetrating critique of both racism and anti-racism can be summarized in a few propositions. First, greed, not ontological racism, is the primary source of injustice generally, and racism specifically: "Capitalist exploitation does not start with ready-made abstractions that first divide the world neatly—by whatever philosophical or theological schematization—between humans and nonhumans. Rather, the process of exploitation produces those distinctions."[191]

Second, the foundational form of injustice is thus class, not race: "it is the persistence and spread of poverty and their antidemocratic antecedents and effects, and their structural and systemic consequences for black life, not the influx of an abstract whiteness, that displaces."[192]

Third, a truly social justice would be centered on the economic, not the psychological and therapeutic: "Replacing identitarian antiracism with an antiracist approach focused on political economy gets us closer to overcoming racism. . . . Relying, as identitarianism increasingly does, on vague concepts like 'whiteness' . . . might be rhetorically useful, but it will not in the end get us very far."[193] Tran is particularly miffed by the broad acceptance of whiteness as a concept given its clear philosophical contradictions, dubious historicity, and abstraction-induced inability to do much more than call for the "abolition of whiteness."[194]

Finally, identitarian anti-racism (what he calls the "orthodox" antiracist view) gets identity wrong by granting race a total determinacy and apparently ontological salience in the formation of identity that it simply does not have:

> [Identitarian antiracism's] intense focus on racial identity severely limits its explanatory power. . . . Racial identity misconstrues identity, and therefore persons, making of identity's translational, provisional, and pragmatic character something essential, permanent, and ideal. Emphasizing race above all other forms of identification—where one's racial identity determines everything about one's identity—then has the effect of misconstruing how identity works altogether.[195]

Tran and Berry's assertions might sound like a flirtation with blasphemy to the orthodox anti-racist ear, but both of them articulate well some of the challenging theses nailed on the door of the reigning anti-racist orthodoxy by aspiring anti-racists who think the orthodoxy needs reforming. And while on the subject of potential blasphemy, throughout the book Berry also commits orthodox anti-racism's unpardonable sin: he invokes the concept of friendship.

FRIENDSHIP

Pastor Florer-Bixler thinks we have made far too much of the power of friendship. She is not alone. In *Divided by Faith*, Michael O. Emerson and Christian Smith detailed how the "white evangelical tool kit" is overly dependent upon instruments of individualism, and how white evangelicals are subsequently drawn to the verifiably false assumption that friendly individual relationships between people of different races would basically solve all our race problems.[196]

As stated earlier in the book, personal friendships cannot by themselves rid the world of systemic injustice. The belief they can is a misguided, destructive, and sadly popular myth, for as Florer-Bixler rightly asserts, "Framing enmity as an issue solely between individuals, rather than dependent upon systemic and coercive power, is popular in and outside the church."[197] Speaking specifically of power inequity in policing, she proclaims "we need a new culture, not relationships, to address this inequity."[198]

So agreed—too much can and often is made of the power of friendship. But could it also be true that while some make too much of how much friendship can do, some make too little of how much friendship can do? Yes, enmity framed in solely individualistic terms is popular in and outside the church, but is not enmity framed in solely systemic terms equally popular in many circles? I once played a drinking game involving a shot of bourbon every time a certain CNN anchor used the word "systemic." Beyond confessing that I remember nothing of the game except that it was played, and I am told I participated, I will plead the fifth.

In the infamous confrontation between a white police officer and a black male, Florer-Bixler has suggested inequity cannot be addressed with personal relationships, but only through a new culture. Going further, she thinks the attempts of police departments to build personal relationships with those they police are not only ineffectual, but distracting and harmful: "Interpersonal connection is an unhelpful distraction. In the hands of police it is propaganda . . . [that] . . . plays on feelings of empathy in order to sidetrack the documented, systemic racism and violence of policing in the United States."[199]

So we need a new culture and not relationships. Fair enough. But of what does a culture consist, fundamentally, if not relationships? Policies? Laws? While we must work without ceasing to discern and implement just policies, it seems mistaken to belittle the role of relationships in the formation of something called "culture." And if we find ourselves believing personal relationships are a categorical distraction and hindrance to the work of justice (in this specific example, as it relates to policing), then surely we find ourselves believing something that is obviously unbelievable.

Returning to that clumsy straight line Berry feels the anti-racists are prone to draw, he asserts that simplistic but claiming-to-be-complex framings of race prevalent in anti-racism are "dissolved by any unpresuming, earnest conversation between a black person and a white person . . . [or] . . . by friendship or affection between a white person and a black person, as they were for me in my childhood and have remained."[200]

Berry makes it clear he has no desire to propose anything like a "solution" to "the race problem," but he must stubbornly denounce the plainly unbelievable (and yet believed by many) belief that friendship is irrelevant or harmful to justice and wholeness:

> . . . some time ago hearing a report on the radio of an angry and somewhat violent confrontation after the killing of a black man by a white police officer, I thought, "Those people don't know each other." That thought was reflexive . . . but it came nevertheless out of my belief, growing over many years, in the importance of people knowing one another, of being willing to know one another, of meeting face-to-face, eye to eye, and speaking to one another, in conversation of course, which I hold to be necessary and precious, but also familiarly in the way of decent manners and goodwill.[201]

I understand that some will find Berry's remarks almost impossibly quaint because many of us think we now know better than believing that knowing each other can make a difference. But Berry is confident that those who think they know better do not know what they think they know. Because knowing each other cannot always make *all* the difference, but maybe it can make *a* difference, and maybe it can *sometimes* make all the difference.

A member of my church who is a friend found himself in a very dangerous situation. He is a young, black male. He has struggled heroically with mental health issues closely connected with some physiological issues well beyond his control. Through a tragic turn of events, he found himself living out of his car. As one might expect, a young, black man living out of and sleeping in his car is a recipe for a complicated situation.

Eventually, I received a phone call about the situation from another member of my church who was a white, male police officer. He informed me that my friend had been frequently acting out in public in extremely erratic fashion, was becoming the source of many complaints, and there loomed the possibility of a confrontation with a police officer. Indeed, the officer was calling me on his way to "the scene" because another officer had come upon my friend asleep in his car and requested backup.

And so this white, male police officer intervened on behalf of this young, black male because, and only because, they had a relationship. He arrived on scene, ensured my friend and his brother in Christ would not be arrested, set him up in a hotel for a week, set him up with desperately needed mental health help, and asked if our church could help him find a more permanent living situation.

I do not tell this story to imply personal relationships are a total solution for the world's systemic problems. They are not. I agree that friendship cannot save the world. I tell it because it is a true story and a reminder that in our attempts to speak of more than friendship we dare not and cannot speak of less than friendship. In this specific and complicated circumstance of race and policing, a personal relationship was not a distraction, but a potential life-or-death matter that proved to be a matter of life. In this specific situation, Wendell Berry was right, which more than implies he is right about more than this specific situation.

EXAGGERATION

An acquired taste that not all will acquire, Berry's writing can seem (forgive me, Wendell) boring. His hot takes are usually agrarian, and topsoil digressions have a marked inability to trend. Florer-Bixler's writing is not boring, and so reading them together is something like binging Twitter/X for reactions to last night's election while also watching smoke signals about the history of tobacco farming in Kentucky.

My own rhetorical instincts are much closer to Florer-Bixler's. I find the well-placed zinger almost irresistible. And, in Florer-Bixler's and my defense, there is a place for zingers. But there being a place for them does not justify an unhealthy reliance upon them, and our promiscuous employment of provocative speech is particularly problematic considering our speech does not just express our thinking but also shapes it. So when our speech becomes untethered from reality, it is not purely provocative; it is false. And provocative but untethered speech goes by the name *exaggeration*.

Exaggeration is not one of the seven deadly sins, but I'm not sure Berry would agree. Our cultural holy wars are in many ways sustained by exaggeration, justified always by the belief that our exaggeration is OK because it's exaggeration for a good cause. The culture wars are premised on that ancient "us versus them" oversimplification, and that oversimplification depends on exaggeration. Exaggeration, according to Berry, "is a violence of language ... extremities of generalization, language overpowering knowledge ..."[202] One struggles to find a more apt description of the reigning rhetorical reality than "language overpowering knowledge."

A great blessing of the general populist shift in modern culture is that many more people now have a voice; a great curse of the general populist shift in modern culture is that many more people now have a voice. And with so many voices competing, exaggeration has proved one of the best ways to stand out. Not completely unlike those colorful feathers that make a bird of paradise a bit more likely to pass on his genes than his less-colorful competitors, exaggeration is incrementally normalized through its many successes. But Berry thinks we should count the costs of exaggeration's success more closely. What do we lose when exaggeration keeps winning?

We face an immediate hurdle in answering this question: chronic exaggerators do not think themselves chronic exaggerators. As mentioned, speech shapes and does not merely express our thinking, which means exaggeration in our speaking leads to exaggeration in our thinking, which leads to even more exaggeration in our speaking because what we once said in knowingly exaggerated rhetoric we now believe to be unexaggerated reality. The line of exaggeration moves ever further. What you once believed to be a B+ you exaggeratingly spoke of as a C to make your point, but your speech eventually led you to believe that the B+ really was a C that you now exaggeratingly speak of as a D to make your point. And so on.

A second hurdle is that we do not like to be accused of exaggeration. One presumes this dislike was always so, but, at risk of exaggeration, there are reasons to believe we might be especially sensitive to accusations of it. Here we bump up against that odd convergence of individualism and relativism wherein we believe in the obvious relativism of all perspectives—except ours. It makes a strange sort of nonsensical sense. If truth is something we impose on reality and not something reality imposes on us, then we're all just making it up as we go, so dogma is whatever I say it is, reality be damned, because I *am* reality. Thus, we are happy to assume the relativity of others' perspectives but offended to the point of grief when the relativity and fallibility of ours is mentioned, and especially so in the context of our modern holy wars.

We must start with the observation that, contrary to a strong and perhaps well-deserved counterpunch being thrown now from the center and right at the far left, exaggeration is not a phenomenon restricted to the left fringe. Indeed, it is no exaggeration to say there has been no more exaggerated and exaggerating person in modern history than Donald Trump. But seeing leftists as an important and fruitful conversation partner, Berry is worried that exaggeration has been allowed to run far too rampant in the current discussions on social justice in progressive circles. Florer-Bixler's case is an interesting one.

In a confession both moving and candid, she says her book was written as a "cantankerous act of love" for her tradition's (Mennonite) inadequate response to the Trump administration.[203] She describes the Trump administration as a reign of terror wherein she was constantly afraid, both for herself and others, because she was terrified by what Trump meant for minorities of all sorts and their allies. As already mentioned, she saw Trump as a phenomenon explicable more or less fully in terms of white supremacy, and that is a terrifying thing to think you are beholding.

I have no question about Pastor Florer-Bixler's sincerity, and I do not think she thinks she is exaggerating, and I know many shared and share her terror. But I do think Berry would suggest that aggregating our situation into a war of terror waged by terrified minorities and their allies against terrifying white supremacists and their witting and unwitting enablers is rhetoric overpowering reality.

Berry takes particular umbrage at our careless use of the word *racism*: "Until recently I too was using that word to refer to the whole phenomenon of race prejudice, but that now seems approximate and unfair. In the course of this writing I have been obliged to consider that race prejudice manifests itself in degrees or intensities too various and numerous to name or know."[204]

He describes prejudice as something that exists on a continuum and not as a binary sorting of racists and anti-racists. This is not to say there are no racists; there are, and we should call them that "with no hesitation at all."[205] But it is to say that most people—including even those who think themselves anti-racist—harbor various forms of prejudice, some of it racial, and rather than calling them *racists*, we speak more truthfully by speaking of prejudice. Furthermore, prejudice is something that exists in degrees and not absolutes. We all harbor various degrees of various prejudices. This is a more accurate moral description of our situation than the rhetorical absolutism of racists vs. anti-racists. And so in rhetoric unexaggerated but still forceful, Berry summarizes his decision to speak judiciously instead of provocatively:

> Certainly it is wrong to label as racists whole categories of people, such as all rural Americans who voted for Trump, or all rural Americans. And so as I have worked my way to here I have been more and more inclined to use the term "racism" only where I am sure it belongs, and elsewhere to replace it with "race prejudice."[206]

Linguist John McWhorter agrees, arguing racism presently has far too many definitions, its meaning now stretched to cover phenomena so morally distant that it is unhelpful for them to share a name: "One of the thorniest aspects of today's race debate is that we have come to apply that word [racism] to a spread of phenomena so vast as to potentially confuse even the best-intended of people."[207] Because if racism means personal bigotry, or systemic inequality even in the absence of personal bigotry, racism would appear to mean too many things to mean anything.

Berry feels the same about our usage of *justice* and affirms Hauerwas's affirmation that it's not clear we know what we mean when we speak of justice. For *justice* is a sacred word, so when we invoke it by its high and holy name, "we had better know clearly and say plainly what we mean by it. It is a word too easy to appropriate for bad purposes. How many wars have not been known by at least one side as 'just' even as both sides have invented new kinds and technologies of injustice?"[208]

Standing in the crowd at a local NAACP event, I once witnessed something like what I imagine a conversation on this matter would be like between Florer-Bixler and Berry. Bennie Walsh, whom I have mentioned previously, is the president of our local NAACP and was reflecting upon how proud he was of the progress he had seen over his many years of racial justice work. He spoke of how grateful he was for the freedom African

Americans now enjoyed. At this point, he was interrupted by a younger black woman in the middle of the crowd, chanting, "We're still not free."

I knew her. She did wonderful work for children in our city, and I had developed a deep respect for her. And in my own limited capacity, I understood what she was saying: there's still so much work to be done; let's not pretend all is well; justice's march must continue. But I happened to be standing beside an older black man who is a friend and a member of my church, and it was immediately apparent he was far less sympathetic to her disruption. While he did not try to silence her, he shook his head as she chanted, obviously troubled. Afterwards I saw him seek her out and watched as they engaged in a firm exchange.

When I saw him the next Sunday, I told him the encounter had struck me as a moment meant to manifest something important and asked if he would be comfortable sharing what had been said. He graciously obliged and, in his understated way, said, "I told her that I agree we have further to go, but we will not get further by exaggerating how far we have not come. She disagreed. She's a good person but she's wrong."

One such flashpoint of exaggeration and its effects can be found in the views people have on policing and race in America. In a 2019 survey, US citizens were asked how many unarmed black American men were killed by the police yearly. Across the ideological spectrum, lots of people had astonishingly exaggerated guesses. Among those who identified themselves as "very liberal," 22 percent guessed it was at least ten thousand a year. Among those who identified as "liberal," almost 40 percent guessed it was at least one thousand a year. And even among those who identified as "very conservative," over 20 percent guessed it was at least one thousand a year.

For 2019, the actual number of unarmed black American men killed by the police was somewhere between ten and thirty.[209] And that is ten to thirty too many, but one has to wonder what role exaggerated rhetoric has played in so stupendously warping our perception of reality on such a critically important matter.

I don't raise this example to suggest all accusations of racial injustice in policing are exaggerated—obviously many are not. I raise it because the killing of unarmed black American men by police was raised up as the quintessential example of racial injustice in policing, which meant it inevitably became a site for the waging of our cultural holy wars, which means it illustrates well the seductive but destructive rationale of righteous exaggeration. An exaggerated example was propped up and then easily knocked down, which tragically increased the skepticism of conservatives in regard to racial injustice in policing. Exaggeration is an illusory rhetorical shortcut that actually always leaves us further from our destination.

Our susceptibility to exaggeration's siren song is related to Daniel Patrick Moynihan's dictum that there's a proportionally inverse relationship between the claims of human rights violations in a country and the actual number of human rights violations in a country. Put simpler, relatively just and free societies produce many claims of injustice and oppression, whereas relatively unjust and oppressive societies produce few claims of injustice and oppression. The more just you are, the more you will be accused of injustice; the less just you are, the less you will be accused of it. The logic of the phenomenon is linear.

For example, compared to most countries, and certainly compared to most countries throughout history, America's treatment of females is, on the whole, incredibly equitable. To choose one of many examples, Iran's treatment of females is not equitable, and it is surely a country begging for a MeToo kind of reckoning. Nobody would claim women are treated more equitably in Iran than in America. But then why are the accusations of misogyny so much louder and more numerous in America than in Iran?

Clearly, the primary reason is not because America is *more* misogynous than Iran but because it is so much *less* misogynous than Iran. For the foreseeable future, no MeToo movement is happening in Iran because the misogyny there is so great it renders such a movement unthinkable, whereas a MeToo movement was thinkable in America because in America, for all its failings, condemning misogyny makes compelling moral sense to us. Summarizing the tendency of relatively just societies to produce people who produce exaggerated claims of injustice, Douglas Murray observes, "Only a very free society would permit—and even encourage—such endless claims about its own iniquities."[210]

Returning to the issue of who is guilty of being too simplistic, one imagines Florer-Bixler would find Berry's critique of progressive exaggeration simplistic, failing to account for the biblical precedent for righteous anger and prophetic fury. Similarly, one assumes she would deny her rhetoric is exaggerated because she finds the justice situation in America to be, simply, racist and oppressive. One imagines that while Berry would agree the justice situation in America includes far too much racism and oppression, he would disagree it is *simply* racist and oppressive. And furthermore, one imagines Berry would find Florer-Bixler's rhetoric an example of oversimplification manifesting as exaggeration.

ANGER

The last specific point of tension that merits mentioning has to be anger. It should be clear that on most of the previous points, I think that while Florer-Bixler and Berry elevate one another when placed in conversation, I also think Berry does more lifting. But on the topic of anger, I confess ignorance as to who provides more lift.

Florer-Bixler once again calls upon the wise and formidable perspective of Willie Jennings to suggest that churches should be places where anger is properly cultivated instead of shunned and suppressed. Like chemotherapy, anger can be a ravaging force of destruction, but when handled wisely that destruction can be in service to the extreme healing that sometimes only extreme measures can bring.

And Jennings's words, shared in reaction to the murder of George Floyd, make the point as well as it can be made. After stating that anger is not only permissible but required in many situations, he provides the important caveat that he knows "it is very dangerous to suggest the connection between human anger and God's indignation" because there is "great danger and great power in saying what I am angry about, God is angry about."[211] So how do we know when the connection is fitting? Jennings provides two answers.

First, our anger is God's when our anger is "about the destruction of life." Anger over injustice qualifies because injustice always destroys life. Second, our anger is God's when it is "shareable." His meaning is less clear here, but at minimum he means that we can trust our anger is God's when our anger can be confirmed, experienced, and taken hold of by others.

By these standards, Jennings is confident that black anger over racial injustice in America is an expression of God's anger, and should be taken hold of by everybody, especially Christians. The failure of many to do so is "one of the most stubborn barriers to overcoming this racial world." Yet while Jennings can be fierce, he is always careful, and he acknowledges that even righteous anger is a thorny nettle to grasp because "anger can easily touch hatred." Certainly the road from righteous anger to un- and self-righteous hatred is wide and many will find it. So how do we avoid that well-trodden path from righteous anger to unrighteous hatred?

Jennings answers, "What Christian faith knows is that the way to keep anger from hatred is not to deny anger, to pretend that it is not real. No, we can't do that. What keeps anger from touching hatred is not the cunning of reason or the power of will. It is simply Jesus." It seems he's suggesting that, paradoxically, anger tends toward hatred when it is denied and suppressed. So we should express instead of suppress our anger, trusting that Jesus can be trusted to stand before and for us, blocking our passage into hatred: "Step into . . . God's own righteous indignation, knowing that God will also invite you to turn away from hatred even as you enter the anger."

Berry is less confident in both our ability to know that our anger is God's, and in anger's ability to serve justice, especially regarding "systemic" situations. Speaking of the residual anger from something like the Civil War, Berry suggests that those, be they Yankees or Confederates, who are perfectly comfortable sitting in a posture of righteous indignation toward "them" are "oversimplifying themselves."[212] Given how tangled and sprawling a problem systemic injustice is (hence calling it "systemic"), can there ever be a simple equating of our anger with God's about it? For if injustice is systemic, can our anger about it be simplistic?

Rather than thinking anger is a path toward either justice or hatred, Berry seems to think anger is a step off a cliff that bottoms out in hatred:

> When I was young and could spare the energy I felt plenty of personal dislike and anger, which I enjoyed very much. I learned eventually that such emotions use up a lot of energy and so are weakening. They also are powerfully distracting. They distort one's sense of what is real and necessary and valuable.
>
> And so I believe I know with enough authority that hate and anger, and the fear that often is involved with them, are the worst of all the motives for work, except maybe for greed. The right motive for work, as I believe I know from experience, is love. Love, to begin with, clears the mind of the oversimplifying, mind-destroying emotions that prepare us to make war.[213]

Whereas Jennings and Florer-Bixler see significant daylight between anger and hatred, Berry sees little. For Berry, anger is less like chemotherapy and more like a lobotomy. Were they to cross-examine each other on anger, I think they would agree it must be expressed instead of suppressed, but they would disagree as to what end anger is expressed. While Florer-Bixler and Jennings feel anger should be expressed so it can be righteously grasped, Berry seems to feel anger should be expressed so it can be righteously released.

Or more accurately, perhaps Florer-Bixler and Jennings feel anger should be expressed so it can be righteously grasped (and sometimes for a long time) so it can be righteously released. I imagine Berry would agree, but caution that since even righteously grasped anger is radioactive, we should limit our exposure to a righteous minimum.

Florer-Bixler believes "communities of reconciliation can emerge out of this anger by identifying a common enemy."[214] Berry believes Florer-Bixler has oversimplified herself and our situation. Jennings believes "God invites us into a shared fury, but only the kind that we creatures can handle." Berry believes we creatures cannot handle shared fury. I do not know who is right, but I believe a transcendent note is struck when their tension is strummed.

THE UNSETTLING OF AMERICA

These five points of tension (Trump, whiteness, friendship, exaggeration, anger) are not exhaustive, but sketch the slant of the divergent angles Florer-Bixler and Berry take on the common problem of injustice and its corollaries. Stepping back, one is left with more of an impression than a prescription, and the impression most impressed upon this reader was the difference in Berry's commitment to think and speak in the most specific and rural terms possible, and Florer-Bixler's commitment to think and speak in terms much more systemic and universal.

Laying his motives and perspective bare in the introduction, Berry agrees America has a systemic injustice problem but disagrees this systemic problem can be dealt with solely systemically, much less through endless big talk about systemic problems and systemic solutions. As mentioned earlier, our problems might be systemic, but our solutions probably aren't. As such, Berry believes generalizations are increasingly causing obfuscation instead of clarification:

> We seem to have agreed to conduct our public conversation about race and racism in terms highly generalized, unexamined, and trite: bare assertions and accusations, generalizations, stereotypes, labels, gestures, slogans, and symbols. This sort of language is useful only to those who see conversation or dialogue as combat, the aim of which is only to win.[215]

Generalizations can be clarifying, but only when they are policed with and for precision, and only when they are the conclusion and not the presupposition. Far too much talking about injustice in America has that distinctly clumsy sound of generalizations asserting themselves loudly in spite of or in the absence of specifics.

Ernest Gaines grew up working on a sugarcane plantation in Louisiana. He eventually made his way to Stanford, where he and Berry met. Gaines was a black novelist, writing candidly and compassionately about race relations in the South, and Berry believes him to be an expert practitioner in the proper use of language. More specifically, Berry thinks Gaines can speak more truthfully than most about race because he speaks so specifically. Gaines uses language located in a small time and place. But instead of being limited by his location, Gaines is expanded by it precisely because he embraces it:

> Because he speaks of and from his own small place, which, as he knows, is only one in a mosaic of thousands of small places, the South cannot be for him an abstract idea as it is for many less settled and located people. Having so particularly placed himself, he cannot speak as a representative southerner any more than he can speak as a representative black person.[216]

So the commitment to speak small and specific makes one's words deep and wide, while the attempt to speak only big and systemic leaves one's words with only a hollow width. But this problem of overly generalized talking is also symptomatic of a deeper problem, which is the overly generalized thinking and living that pervades modern culture. For as Berry sees it, systemic injustice is not merely sustained by race, gender, or sexual prejudice, but by a "prejudice against community life itself."[217]

His contention, upon which most of his work is premised, is that rather than "settling," we have increasingly "unsettled" America. We are an unsettled people incapable of living communal lives because we instead irresistibly gravitate toward the polarities of individualism and cosmopolitanism. On the one hand, I am the center of reality and arbiter of all authority. On the other hand, I am a global citizen who lives in and is responsible for "the world." And so we live lives that are both overly individualistic and overly public.

Situated between the individualistic and the public is the hollowed-out center of modern American life: the local community. It is the context for a proper human life. Scripture and nature tell us so. This does not mean local communities are all gardens of Eden. It does mean they are the spaces—the only spaces—in time where life can be lived as intended. When a local community serves as the home base for our ventures out into the individualistic and public, we can remain whole. But when we venture out into the individualistic and public in search of a home, we wander forever lost and homeless. And so Berry asks,

> What has happened to the families and communities whose expectations and restraints, never public, grew directly from the circumstances and needs of people living together? We need to ask, not because families and communities were ever perfect by their own standards, but because the public and the government are incomplete and in some ways useless when families and communities have disintegrated. When individual people no longer have access to, and are unreachable from, those older forms of local authority, it seems inevitable that a personal wrong or wound may fester for years in some solitary heart until it bursts out at last nakedly in public . . .[218]

According to Berry's thesis, a society without strong local communities would devolve into an anti-society of isolated individuals who hurl accusations, grievances, and insults at each other in public, and think this moral circus constitutes politics and the pursuit of justice.

In the preface to *How to Have an Enemy*, Florer-Bixler claims a perspective that is not completely dissimilar to Berry's—she is a Mennonite pastor who is "a localist when it comes to church" and who doesn't "have an agenda for society at large."[219] This is part of the reason her book stands out in the crowded marketplace of anti-racist works seeking to set white conservative Christians straight. It is clear Florer-Bixler belongs to a church and not merely a Twitter/X cohort. It is clear Florer-Bixler does not want to claim to be *the press secretary for the Trinity and/or the platonic ideal of justice*, unlike many progressive inquisitors. But, as documented above, she is also very drawn to thinking and talking big—or in the parlance nowadays more common, she is drawn to thinking and talking mostly *systemically*.

THE MAN WHO KNEW TOO LITTLE?

Decades back, one of my parishioners had Wendell Berry as a professor at the University of Kentucky. He remembered Berry quite fondly, so when I once mentioned Berry in a sermon, he felt compelled to write Berry and tell him about it and asked if Berry would be kind enough to send me an "autographed" picture. Given that he had not spoken to Berry in decades and had no address for him, the entire endeavor seemed doomed to fail. But nevertheless, he sent a letter with Wendell Berry's name on it to the post office in Port Royal, Kentucky.

To his great surprise, the letter found its way to Berry, and Berry did indeed respond by sending a package. Inside the package there was a short, kind letter in which Berry thanked his former student for writing but informed him he could not send a signed picture of himself because he had no pictures of himself to give away. So instead of a picture, he was sending me—his modern, millennial pastor fanboy—a copy of one of his books, aptly titled, *Why I Am Not Going to Buy a Computer*.

I smiled when I surveyed the package. This is what Wendell Berry would send when asked for an autograph. I thought about how much this man who has lived for so many years on a farm in rural Kentucky (without a computer!) must not know. But as I read his five-hundred-page reflection on prejudice and patriotism, it became clear there was a connection between how much Berry does not know and how much he does know.

Reading Berry, you get the sense he knows more than most because he tries to know less than most. He does not aspire to be a citizen of the world; he aspires to be a citizen of Port Royal, Kentucky. He has narrowed the aperture of his mind down to the small slice of reality to which he actually belongs. But, dialectically, his is a narrow-mindedness that somehow manages to also be capacious; unlike that strange species of modern open-mindedness that somehow manages to be more parochial than (one imagines) Neanderthal politics.

Somewhat similar to the accusation that many affluent white people make a universal norm out of affluent white culture because they fail to understand it as one particular culture among many others, Berry contends that the more cosmopolitan thinking currently in vogue in professional intellectual culture unwittingly norms cosmopolitan thinking as universal thinking instead of seeing it as one narrow way to think among many others. What Berry calls his commitment to "the country way of seeing" has the advantage of knowing it is narrow, whereas the cosmopolitan gaze has the severe disadvantage of imagining itself to not be narrow.

As exhibit A, Berry calls attention to *The New York Times*. A leader in cosmopolitan thinking, it consistently exhibits the tendency to think that the world as experienced in urbane New York City circles is the world properly experienced. Berry's critique of columnist Paul Krugman's metropolitan arrogance is especially amusing. According to Krugman, there are two Americas: real America and rural America. Real America is metropolitan, educated, diverse. Rural America is "non-college whites."[220]

This notion that metropolitan life is *real* life and every other kind of life is something *other than* real life pervades an institution like *The Times*. Columnist Farhad Manjoo is another example of a perspective so parochial but thinking itself universal it almost reads as satire:

> Creating dense, urban environments ought to be a paramount goal of progressivism. Dense urban areas are quite literally "the real America"—the cities are where two-thirds of Americans live, and they account for almost all national economic output. They're good for the environment. . . . Finally, metropolises are good for the psyche and the soul; density fosters diversity, creativity and progress.[221]

Dense urban environments are good for the environment? They're good for the psyche and soul? They are, literally, the real America? The fact that Manjoo apparently thinks there are no dots to connect between the unsettling of America, the invention of racial capitalism, mass migration to cities, looming environmental collapses, economic injustice, and epidemics of loneliness and anxiety is, if nothing else, impressively naïve. The unsettling of America manifested in the urbanization of America is, in Manjoo's mind, progress, pure and simple. Berry thinks the march toward the metropolis in our thinking, talking, and living is neither pure nor simple.

Thinking, talking, and living "systemically" and at a global scale is a hallmark of progressive ideology, which sees such systemic thinking, talking, and living as the cure for injustice. It is a sincere belief, but Wendell Berry would like us to consider if this alleged cure is actually a cause. In sum, Berry believes the very attempt to think and talk so relentlessly systemically about injustice perpetuates injustice because it perpetuates the unsettling of America that is our deepest wound.

Florer-Bixler and Berry have both given us a needed word, to which I have added a few of my own and a few of others, in the hopes their mingling might pull us up, if only a little, into the transcendent symphony that is God.

9

Twenty-Six Names
Are You Better than Them?

THE MOST FAMOUS LETTER ever written closes by mentioning twenty-six names.

Paul often ended a letter with a string of names and greetings, but what we find in Romans is excessive, even for him. More names are mentioned and greetings bestowed in the final chapter of Romans than in all his other letters combined. There's much to learn from these twenty-six names.

Many are female. Given Paul appears to be greeting leaders, it appears women led prominently in Rome's early churches. Thoroughly unimpressed with equality, ancient Roman society found early Christianity's insistence on the inclusion and equality of women silly and shameful. The spirit of the age was not in the church's sails when it came to women. Nor slaves. Several slave names are mentioned in Romans 16 as well, and having slaves in membership, much less leadership, was a similar faux pas.

There are Greek names, Latin names, and Jewish names.

These twenty-six names—male and female, slave and free, rich and poor, educated and uneducated, Greek and Latin and Jewish—mark a miracle. God in Christ had done something that both affirmed and transcended the foundational gender, class, ethnicity, religion, and ideology identity markers, and summoned an impossibly diverse constituency into a common family.

Both the affirmation and transcendence of identity were important. Take Paul. Paul was born and died a Jew. He often affirmed his Jewishness.[222]

He did not believe Christ erased all difference into sameness but that Christ abolished privilege and demanded an allegiance that transcended all other allegiances. This affirmation-and-transcendence of identity was clearly difficult to sort. What parts of identity should stay? What parts might need to go? What parts could stay or go depending upon the needs and identities of others in the ecclesial family? Contrary to popular belief, Romans is not Paul's grand systematic theology but a specific work of pastoral theology in which he is trying to work out the miracle worked out by God in Christ in real time in the house churches of first-century Rome.

As Scot McKnight suggests, Paul's pastoral focus becomes clear when we "read Romans backwards" and see that all the seemingly speculative theologizing in the first half of the book is in service to a simple to state but hard to embody goal that's revealed at the end of the book: "Greet one another with a holy kiss" (Rom 16:16).

Ancient Roman Christians were far more affectionate and less prudish than we are, but this was still difficult counsel. Embracing others as family sounds nice but is hell to live because others can be awful. And while not quite the clown show of the church in Corinth, the house churches of Rome were filled with people who found one another more than a little difficult to greet with a holy kiss. Yet God in Christ had done something to gather this impossibly diverse family, and it was their duty to be the family Christ claimed they already were.

WEAK AND STRONG

Weak and strong—this is Paul's shorthand description for the two groups whose conflict appears to have occasioned Paul's grand letter. Not everyone fit cleanly into these two groups, and one's placement surely existed more on a continuum than in an either/or box, but Paul believes the description is accurate enough to describe the conflict. So who are the weak, who are the strong, and why are they in conflict?

About fifteen years before Romans was written, most Jews and Jewish Christians were expelled from Rome by Claudius. When Claudius died, the expelled were allowed to return, and this return happened just before Paul wrote Romans.

Imagine how much had changed in those fifteen years. Imagine how different the Roman house churches had become. The earliest Christian churches were filled with and led by Jewish Christians, and while they made room for gentiles, they expected gentiles to fit in. Jesus was for everyone, but the Jewish Christians were still accustomed to a gatekeeping role. Fifteen years later, their role had been filled in their absence, and they returned to find churches that are now filled with and mostly led by gentile Christians. It might not have been Dean Wormer stepping into the Delta Tau Chi fraternity house, but it must have been troubling. This brings us back to our three questions, better equipped to answer them.

The weak are primarily Jewish Christians who believe Jesus is the Messiah but also believe faithfulness to Yahweh still requires strict Torah observance. As a result, they are judgmental of the loose, libertarian gentiles who are new to God's family and don't know how to behave. The strong are primarily gentiles who believe Jesus is Lord but don't believe in the necessity of strict Torah observance. Therefore, they are contemptuous of the prissy, moralizing Jewish Christians.[223] The nature of their conflict is plain and eternal: they agree we should follow Jesus; they disagree how.

With only a bit of anachronism, we might say the weak manifest the conservative spirit, alive in the world since the second man carried on the traditions of the first. And the strong manifest the progressive spirit, alive in the world since the third man decided his father and grandfather didn't know everything about everything.

Like a tsunami that has built on its approach to shore, Paul's heady theologizing breaks upon the Romans in a merciful but severe torrent of pastoral admonition in chapters 14–15. He starts with a strong word for the strong: "The one who eats is not to regard with contempt the one who does not eat . . ." (Rom 14:3a). Contempt is the temptation of the strong. You are enlightened, progressive, ahead of history's curve. You eat the bacon. You do not suffer conservative fools. The contempt feels good, and you have good grounds for it. But Paul disagrees. Your contempt is sin, and you need to repent.

Next up is a strong word for the weak: ". . . and the one who does not eat is not to judge the one who eats, for God has accepted him" (Rom 14:3b). Judgment is the temptation of the weak. You are responsible, conservative, faithful to heritage. You do not eat the bacon. You do not cave to progressive loons. The judgment feels right and is surely righteousness. But Paul disagrees. Your judgment is sin, and you need to repent.

Lest they've missed his point, Paul repeats himself: "But you, why do you judge your brother? Or you again, why do you regard your brother with contempt? For we will all stand before the judgment seat of God" (Rom 14:10).

So if you fancy yourself a progressive fellow, your assignment is not the enlightenment of the conservative but contrition for your condescension. And if you pride yourself in being conservative, your assignment is not the judgment of the progressive but the penance of a prig.

Painful and fair enough, but how does Paul ultimately adjudicate this conflict? To eat the bacon or not eat the bacon?

Preceded by his uncompromising, extremist reputation, history has done Paul the disservice of obfuscating what a remarkably laid-back and open-minded man he obviously was. Were it not overly distressing to many readers, one might even suggest the chances that any of us are more laid-back and open-minded than the apostle are nil. This is not to say he was a man without conviction, and on the matter of the bacon at hand, Paul had a conviction and stated it: "I know and am convinced in the Lord Jesus that nothing is unclean in itself..." (Rom 14:14).

Paul's conviction is firm, flexed with a double emphatic: he knows and is convinced in the Lord Jesus that he can eat the bacon. He casts his lot with the strong, explicitly so in 15:1: "Now we who are strong..."

Given such decidedness, Paul's modest arbitration is strange. In 14:5–23, he meanders through a comically indirect proposal, refusing to put his foot down one way or the other. The first couple of verses testify to the vacillation that follows:

> One person regards one day above another, another regards every day alike. Each person must be fully convinced in his own mind. He who observes the day, observes it for the Lord, and he who eats, does so for the Lord, for he gives thanks to God; and he who eats not, for the Lord he does not eat, and gives thanks to God. (Rom 14:5–6)

Translation: Eat the bacon! Or don't eat the bacon. Because God knows I'd like to eat the bacon (and am convinced in the Lord I can!), but I understand you might be convinced I can't. And so if you feel that strongly about the bacon, then I won't eat it (or at least won't eat it around you) because the only thing I like more than eating bacon is eating with you. So eat the bacon, or don't eat the bacon. Whatever. Who cares what you eat or don't eat so long as you eat together.

Paul was a man of enormous conviction; after all, he was beaten, shipwrecked, tortured, and murdered for it. So it's impossible he is waffling on the matter of convictions in general, advocating for their abandonment in the name of harmony. So rather than advocating for the abandonment of deep conviction in the name of the harmonious good, Paul is advocating for two of his deepest convictions.

First, be wary of mistaking your convictions for God's. Second, your deepest conviction must be embracing those of different convictions in Christ. Why? Because that's what God in Christ did with you: "Welcome one another, therefore, just as Christ has welcomed you, for the glory of God" (Rom 15:7, NRSV). This welcome does not require you to abandon your convictions, but that you submit all of them to the supreme conviction that God in Christ has welcomed everybody—even you; even *them*.

But perhaps this sounds petty and inconsequential to a modern mind; the unenlightened quarrelling of ancient people who were superstitious about food and ignorant about equality. They needed Paul's reconciling admonition, but our situation is much more dire and complicated. We have *ideological* differences, and as documented earlier, reconciling admonitions allegedly cannot apply here. Too much is at stake.

Such rationale is typical of modern anachronistic arrogance. Our divisions are much more serious; our justifications much more righteous—so we tell ourselves. But this is pompous nonsense. No, our divisions are not more serious, nor our justifications more righteous. Considering the modern world, despite its many flaws, is indisputably more compassionate, just, and equitable than the biblical world, it's most certain that our divisions are less serious, our justifications less righteous.

If anything, Paul's reconciling admonition applies even more so to us. In fact, maybe God chose the Jew/gentile conflict as the occasion in history to display the reconciling power of the gospel because it was one of the most irreconcilable conflicts in human history and would thus render all our excuses impotent. Because if Paul can ask the Jew and gentile to get over themselves to make room for each other just as God in Christ had done for them, what makes us think we can escape a similar subpoena? This brings us back to the beginning of Romans, and the theological foundation laid there: the orthodoxy supporting this towering orthopraxy.

YOU PRACTICE THE SAME THINGS

They are filled with unrighteousness, wickedness, greed, evil, envy, murder, strife, deceit, and malice. They are slanderers, haters of God, and inventors of evil.

Paul's bleak summarization of unbelieving people in the latter half of Romans 1 is often mistaken for a universalizing description of sinful humanity writ large, as if this is what Paul thinks all humanity is like without Christ. But with Paul's reconciling end in mind, we can see the clever rhetorical trap he is setting. As noted by McKnight, Paul's vicious portrayal of sinners in Romans 1:18–32 is clearly tapping into a deep Jewish stereotype about the degeneracy of *gentile* sinners.[224] Because while Jews knew they sinned, they also knew gentiles were the worst of all sinners. James Dunn puts it like this: "They do not sin like the Gentiles, or if they do, their sin is not so serious. Thus, Israel is disciplined, but others are punished. Israel is chastised, but others are scourged. Israel is tested, but the ungodly are condemned. Israel expects mercy, but their opponents can look only for wrath."[225]

So rather than expressing his true thoughts on all humanity, Paul is here throwing out red meat, leaning into the caricature, surfacing all the spite, eliciting the full measure of Jewish disgust for gentile sinners. The Jewish Christians in the room are surely grinning from ear to ear as Phoebe reads this part of Paul's letter, happier than a Republican listening to Tucker Carlson. Though notorious among the conservative Jewish Christians for his liberal embrace of gentiles, Paul has here endeared himself to the right side of the room because he said what they have all been thinking. Yes! Gentile sinners are the worst, and these gentile Christians little better. Make the Roman churches more Jewish again!

Having drawn the seething sum of Jewish spite and self-righteousness out into the open, the blow Paul then deals is devastating: "Therefore you have no excuse, everyone of you who passes judgment, for in that which you judge another, you condemn yourself; for you who judge practice the same things" (Rom 2:1).

We practice the same things?

The same things as the gentiles?

The slanderous, God-hating, evil-inventing gentiles?

I like to think Phoebe's public reading of Romans was interrupted at this point by a barrage of boisterous rebuttals and accusations. How dare Paul equivocate Jewish and gentile sin? How dare Paul play both sides? Phoebe lets them vent their complaints, then continues reading. Paul has anticipated it all, and rather than back down, he will lean further in: "And we know that the judgment of God rightly falls upon those who practice such things. But do you suppose this, O man, when you pass judgment on those who practice such things and do the same yourself, that you will escape the judgment of God?" (Rom 2:2–3).

We like to think of ourselves as unique in our struggles, as people who do sin but don't do the worst sins. If you're conservative, you do sin, but you don't do the progressive sins: vote Democrat, play the victim, make everything about race or gender or sexuality, water down orthodoxy when explaining it to your agnostic barista who we all know you're never actually going to explain orthodoxy to. If you're progressive, you do sin, but you don't do the conservative sins: vote Republican, blame the victim, be a racist, chauvinist, homophobe, mistake American manifest destiny for the Apostles' Creed.

Paul does not see it this way. While attuned to sin's many manifestations, Paul thinks these spring from a few common forms that are more consequential than the subsequent manifestations. Down at the root, all sin begins to look similar. We steal, we hoard, we lust, we lie, we boast, we judge. We practice the same things. Our sin is not special.

To the consternation of his well-meaning but misguided Jewish Christian comrades in the room, Paul refuses to give an inch. There are no grounds whatsoever for Jewish superiority. Or gentile superiority. There is no partiality with God, no moral superiority among men.

ARE WE BETTER THAN THEM?

The room is quiet now. Not because everyone agrees with what Paul has said, but because all can feel the weight of it. Paul is on a theological high wire. Will he fall?

To one side there is God's election of Israel; to deny it is to deny the faith. To the other side there is God's inclusion of gentiles; to deny it is to deny the gospel.

As chapter three begins, Paul affirms God's election of Israel. It is real and carries privileges. He will elaborate further on them in 9:4–5, but here he wants to affirm that Israel got to steward God's promises (Rom 3:1–2). Their fidelity to that stewardship, however, was a mixed bag, and, according to Paul, Israel failed to keep Torah and to share God's promises with the nations. This begs the question of whether Israel's failure is also God's failure, of whether Israel's unfaithfulness to God implies God's unfaithfulness to Israel.

This is a difficult but simple question for Paul. Because while God freely accepts responsibility for Israel's infidelity, Paul knows he cannot take it a step further and believe God's voluntary responsibility for Israel's infidelity entails God's culpability for it. So all of Paul's complicated reasoning is anchored in a simple, immovable conviction: God cannot be unfaithful. Given that God cannot be unfaithful, the only possible answer to the question of who is culpable for Israel's infidelity is Israel. To suggest otherwise is not edgy, but incompetent (Rom 3:4–8).

Thus, we are led to another question in verse 9. It's tough to say if it's the most important question Paul asks in Romans, but it's certainly the question provoking most of what has been said in this book. It's a single word question in Greek: *proexometha*. We can frame it up a few ways:

Are we more excellent?
Are we better?
Are we any better off?
Are we worse off?
Are we better than them?

Whom do you despise? Whom do you *most* despise? Maybe a lover who betrayed you, a friend who wounded you, a guardian who abused you, a boss who belittled you, a stranger who hurt you. Maybe a group of people you're convinced is ruining your community, or your church, or the country, or the world. We all have a *them*. With *them* in mind, hear Paul's question: are you better than them?

Hell, yes, I am. Don't get me wrong; I know I'm a sinner. I need constant forgiveness for the things I have done and left undone. I am banking on mercy I do not and could never demand. But yeah, I am better. I have a few thems. I genuinely hate some of them. I think you'd hate them too. But I'm sure my thems aren't nearly as bad as some of yours. I've never experienced something I think rises to the level of radical abuse. Many have. Are you better than your thems?

Not at all. (Rom 3:9b.)

At risk of understatement, this is an outrageous assertion. You are not better than them? You are not better than the person who radically wronged you? You are not better than the groups who oppose everything (you think) God stands for?

It's perhaps the hardest of Scripture's hard truths: *ou pantos* in Greek— not at all. Then Paul piles on.

There is no righteous person, not even one;

> There is no one who understands,
> There is no one who seeks out God;
> They have all turned aside, together they have become corrupt;
> There is no one who does good,
> There is not even one. (Rom 3:10–11, NASB 2020)

A more comprehensive indictment would be hard to find. When we reach anthropological bedrock, the categories awaiting us are not victim and oppressor, nor devotee and heretic, but guilty and not guilty. The sorting is simple: we are all guilty; Christ is not. Other categories can and must then be constructed, but only upon this foundation, and never as *the* foundation. There are only sinners. You are not better than them.

THE JUDGE JUDGED IN OUR PLACE

The bad news is worse than we thought, but to whatever degree the bad news is bad, the good news is better. The good news is the only person fit to judge anybody is the Christ who has already judged everybody, and judged everybody guilty but forgiven because they are loved. Nobody has said this better than Barth in "The Judge Judged in Our Place":

> It is a nuisance, and at bottom at intolerable nuisance, to have to be the man who gives sentence. It is a constraint always to have to be convincing ourselves that we are innocent, we are in the right....
>
> We are all in the process of dying from this office of judge which we have arrogated to ourselves. It is, therefore, a liberation that it has come to pass in Jesus Christ that we are deposed and dismissed from this office because He has come to exercise it in our place....
>
> It is no longer necessary that I should pronounce myself free and righteous. It is no longer necessary that even if only in my heart I should pronounce others guilty. Neither will help either me or them in the very least. Whatever may be the answer to the question of their life and mine, at any rate it no longer needs to be given by me. To find it and to pronounce it is no longer my office or in any way my concern. I am not the Judge. Jesus Christ is Judge. The matter is taken out of my hands. And that means liberation....
>
> He who knows about myself and others as I never could or should do, will judge concerning me and them in a way which is again infinitely more just than I could ever do—and judge and decide in such a way that it will be well done.... And whatever the decision may be, I have reason to look forward to its disclosure with terror, but with a terror-stricken joy.[226]

The truth is often more of a challenge to true believers than straightforward foes, more challenging to those who think they've accepted it than even those who actively oppose it. The challenge is especially challenging when dealing with truths that are, by their nature, denied when we imagine them mastered. The truth of the gospel is such a truth. We deny it when we suppose we have mastered it. There is no greater betrayal of the gospel than the belief that we are better than they are, but it's a belief we Christians are especially susceptible to when the justice of the gospel takes hold of us. Because we want to set the world right. We need to set the world right. We've seen our sin, and we have to make them see their sin, for the common good. But the wisdom of the ages is undeniable: our zeal for justice and righteousness is so easily compromised by judgment and self-righteousness.

Jesus can wield the whip righteously, but can you? Your assurance you can is likely assurance you can't. As Volf has said, the precondition of properly imitating Christ is remembering you are not Christ.[227] Similarly, our claims to be imitating Christ often far outrun the actual language of Scripture because imitating Christ is not a general, vague concept, but a specific command whose specific reference is the crucifixion.[228] In other words, we often claim Messiah-precedent when asserting ourselves upon others for justice's sake (i.e., wielding the whip righteously), but Scripture's many admonitions to follow the Messiah's precedent run in the exact opposite direction (i.e., bearing the cross humbly). I don't know if Neil Young knew that he knew this, but he did.

THE REPENTANCE OF NEIL YOUNG

> Well I heard Mr. Young sing about her
> Well I heard ol' Neil put her down
> Well I hope Neil Young will remember
> A southern man don't need him around.

I am Christian first and Texan close second. Texans do not consider ourselves "southern" so much as Texan, but if you grow up Texan you grow up listening to the South's anthem, "Sweet Home Alabama," often, and doing so with a certain sense of pride. But it was years of listening before I realized the second verse documented a conflict between Lynyrd Skynyrd and Neil Young.

Neil Young was a northern man—a Canadian creative destined to be liberal. His enemy was inevitable: the South. It stood for all he stood against, and because Young was the kind of guy driven to stand up for what he stands for, the world would know about it.

It started with "Southern Man," a song featured on one of Young's finest albums, *After the Gold Rush*. As Neil saw and sang it, the "Southern Man" was the racist man, plain and simple. Neil then doubled down on his next album with "Alabama," a song scolding the South for being poor, racist, unjust, unable to get it together.

Ronnie Van Zant loved Neil Young. He was Lynyrd Skynyrd's leader, the southern frontman of a southern band, and Neil was a hero. Van Zant would even wear Neil Young T-shirts while performing. This made Young's blanket condemnations of "the South" especially hurtful to Van Zant and the band. As he told *Rolling Stone*, "We thought Neil was shooting all the ducks in order to kill one or two. We're southern rebels, but more than that, we know the difference between right and wrong."[229] And in the second verse of "Sweet Home Alabama," Van Zant returned fire.

Shakey was shook. One of the most iconic songs of the century had taken dead aim and nailed him. Young then did the most outrageous thing: he repented.

Apologizing for both "Southern Man" and "Alabama," Young admitted "Sweet Home Alabama" was a great song, and he deserved the shot Skynyrd delivered with it. And when he listened to his songs, and what he'd before believed prophetic and righteous lyrics, he no longer liked what he heard: "I don't like my words when listen to it. They are accusatory and condescending, not fully thought out, and too easy to misconstrue."[230]

Young's repentance facilitated reconciliation with Skynyrd. Tragically, they did not have long to walk in it because Van Zant and most members of the band died in a plane crash a few years later. But Young would continue to walk in it on his end, and weeks after their death, Young surprised his fans at a show by playing a medley of "Alabama" and "Sweet Home Alabama" as a tribute to his enemies turned friends. Rumor has it Jesus sang along.

US FOR THEM

How do we pursue God's justice without usurping God's office of judge? The question is ancient but resurfacing with holy menace in our time. We should welcome it. It's a sacred question. In the end, it is not a question that can be settled but only lived more or less faithfully. And to that end, a proposal that presents itself is modest but firm: you've been commanded to be *for* them, even when standing against them, which is tough to do when believing you're better than them.

Justice + Friendship.
Communion > Victory.
Aufhenbung > Schadenfreude.
Left or Right or Middle? Up.
Us ~~VERSUS~~ FOR Them!

Endnotes

CHAPTER ONE

1. Most notably, see Jesse Singal's analysis of this in *The Quick Fix: Why Fad Psychology Can't Cure Our Social Ills*, 173–210.
2. Taylor, *Secular Age*, 706.
3. Sacks, *Morality*, 2.
4. Lohfink, *Does God Need the Church?*, 298–99.
5. hooks, *Outlaw Culture*, 76.
6. Williams, *Dostoyevsky: Language, Faith, and Fiction*, 50.
7. Parker, "Episode 389: How to Make Meetings," 34:21.
8. Smiley, "One Single Thing," para. 3.
9. King, "Letter from a Birmingham Jail," para. 19.
10. Busch, *Karl Barth*, 304.
11. Berry, *World-Ending Fire*, 162–63.
12. Sacks, *Morality*, 317.
13. Sacks, *Morality*, 318.
14. Berry, *Need to Be Whole*, 24.
15. Busch, *Karl Barth*, 323–24.
16. Hauerwas, *Work of Theology*, 18.
17. Volf, *Exclusion and Embrace*, 216.
18. Volf, *Exclusion and Embrace*, 220.
19. Jennings, *After Whiteness*, 146–49.
20. Jennings, *After Whiteness*, 129.
21. Williams, *Looking East in Winter*, 192.
22. Williams, *Looking East in Winter*, 193.
23. Gutiérrez, *Theology of Liberation*, xxxviii.
24. Klein, *Why We're Polarized*, 175.
25. Hauerwas, *After Christendom?*, 50–58. Hauerwas explores Pannenberg's contention that Gutierrez and other liberation theologians, for all their talk of justice, lack a thick account of the actual substance of justice. Hauerwas then apes Pannenberg's critique but ultimately agrees that liberation theology has a justice problem. Hauerwas would define that problem as liberation theology's tendency to be too beholden to modernity's emphasis on autonomy and rights.
26. Volf, *Exclusion and Embrace*, 221.
27. Hauerwas, *After Christendom?*, 45.

28. Hauerwas, *After Christendom?*, 46.
29. Hauerwas, *After Christendom?*, 68.
30. Dostoyevsky, *Brothers Karamazov*, 318.
31. Rutledge, *Crucifixion*, 323.

CHAPTER TWO

32. Blythe, *To Hate Like This Is to Be Happy Forever.*
33. "2020 Democratic Party presidential primaries," see "Withdrew before the primaries" graphic.
34. Klein, *Why We're Polarized*, 63–64.
35. Ryan, *Civilized to Death*, 13.
36. Brueggemann, *Genesis*, 55.
37. Dostoyevsky, *Brothers Karamazov*, 44. Emphasis mine.
38. Bregman, *Utopia for Realists*, 1.
39. Ryan, *Civilized to Death*, 9.
40. Ryan, *Civilized to Death*, 32.
41. Up from around 30 percent in the 1950s. See Lynn Vavreck's *New York Times* article, "A Measure of Identity: Are You Wedded to Your Party?" Similar studies have yielded similar results. See, for example, Klein, *Why We're Polarized*, 75.
42. Klein, *Why We're Polarized*, 76.
43. Iyengar and Westwood, "Fear and Loathing," 690–707.
44. Klein and Chang, "Political Identity Is Fair Game," para. 38.
45. Simmons, "Sarah Silverman on 'Funny' in 2019," 10:45.
46. Yoder, *War of the Lamb*, 60.
47. Minogue, *Liberal Mind*, 1.
48. Cone, *For My People*, 87.

CHAPTER THREE

49. Lohfink wonders the same: "There is a good deal of evidence that Jesus chose the Twelve from the most diverse groups in the Judaism of his time . . ." *Does God Need the Church?*, 174.
50. Leithart, *End of Protestantism*, 16–17.
51. Eph 1:22–23.
52. Quoted in Bishop, *Big Sort*, 19.
53. Wasserman, "Purple America," para. 2. The 2020 election saw the percentage drop slightly below 60 percent, which is encouraging but tough to discern due to the oddness of the election (pandemic, Trump).
54. Quoted in Bishop, *Big Sort*, 23.
55. See *Open versus Closed*, by Christopher Johnston, Christopher Federico, and Howard Lavine; *Prius or Pickup?*, by Marc Hetherington and Jonathan Weiler; *The Righteous Mind*, by Jonathan Haidt; or *Predisposed*, by John Hibbing, Kevin Smith, and John Alford.
56. Klein, *Why We're Polarized*, 231.

Endnotes

57. Quoted in Bishop, *Big Sort*, 35.
58. Klein, *Why We're Polarized*, 167.
59. Harari, *Homo Deus*, 350.
60. Harari, *Homo Deus*, 339.
61. Bishop, *Big Sort*, 22. Turns out Democrats prefer cats and Republicans prefer dogs.
62. Tolentino, *Trick Mirror*, 22.
63. Cited in Klein, *Why We're Polarized*, 148.
64. Klein, *Why We're Polarized*, 149.
65. Klein, *Why We're Polarized*, 160–61.
66. While statistics on ideological sorting within denominations are available they are unhelpful because people do not attend denominations; people attend actual, local churches. And stats on ideological sorting within churches are virtually nonexistent.
67. Berry, *World-Ending Fire*, 216.
68. Luke 5:31–32.
69. Boulton, *Life in God*, 229–30.
70. 1 Cor 9:26–27.

CHAPTER FOUR

71. Lohfink, *Does God Need the Church?*, 27.
72. Hauerwas, *After Christendom*, 44.
73. Ryan, *Civilized to Death*, 169.
74. Heath, *Enlightenment 2.0*, 100.
75. West, *Scale*, 303–304.
76. West, *Scale*, 307.
77. "Census Bureau Releases New Estimates," para. 4 and Beaton, "Why Millennials are Lonely," para. 2.
78. Klein, *Why We're Polarized*, 59.
79. Gottfried von Herder, quoted by Sacks, *Morality*, 133.
80. Berry, *World-Ending Fire*, 228–29.
81. Berry, *World-Ending Fire*, 231.
82. Obama, "How to Make this Moment," para. 6 and 7.
83. Jennings, *Christian Imagination*, 294.
84. Jennings, *Christian Imagination*, 293.
85. Klein, *Why We're Polarized*, 265.
86. Dostoyevsky, *Brothers Karamazov*, 57.
87. Brown, *Braving the Wilderness*. See chapter 4, "People Are Hard to Hate Up Close. Move In."
88. Williams, *Dostoyevsky*, 182–83.
89. Williams, *Dostoyevsky*, 24.
90. Williams, *Dostoyevsky*, 183.
91. Teresa, "Acceptance Speech," para. 12.
92. Williams, *Way of St Benedict*, 27.
93. Williams, *Way of St Benedict*, 18–19.
94. Williams, *Way of St Benedict*, 27–28.
95. Rogan, "Joe Rogan Experience #1595—Ira Glasser," 63:00.

96. Williams, *Way of St Benedict*, 22.
97. Berry, *World-Ending Fire*, 10–11.
98. Berry, *World-Ending Fire*, 13.
99. Berry, *World-Ending Fire*, viii.
100. Berry, *World-Ending Fire*, 327, 330.
101. Dostoyevsky, *Brothers Karamazov*, 26.
102. Hauerwas, *Peaceable Kingdom*, 150.
103. Watts, *Spider-Man: Far From Home*.
104. Berry, *World-Ending Fire*, x.

CHAPTER FIVE

105. Hart, *Theological Territories*, 244.
106. Volf, *Exclusion and Embrace*, 219.
107. Campbell and Manning, *Rise of Victimhood*, 12–16.
108. Murray, *Madness of Crowds*, 252.
109. Pluckrose and Lindsay, *Cynical Theories*, 71.
110. Solzhenitsyn, *Gulag Archipelago*, 312.
111. Solzhenitsyn, *Gulag Archipelago*, 313.
112. Berry, *World-Ending Fire*, 50.
113. Volf, *Exclusion and Embrace*, 105.
114. Volf, *Exclusion and Embrace*, 9.
115. Volf, *Exclusion and Embrace*, 114.
116. McCaulley, *Reading While Black*, 93.
117. Volf, *Exclusion and Embrace*, 117.
118. Volf, *Exclusion and Embrace*, 104.
119. Volf, *Exclusion and Embrace*, 103.
120. Leithart, "Clashing Victimocracies," para. 10.
121. Klein, *Why We're Polarized*, 119.
122. Sacks, *Morality*, 1. Related is his description of modern politics as "a new phenomenon . . . political campaigning focused . . . on a series of self-identifying minorities, leading to the counter-politics of populism on behalf of a beleaguered and enraged native-born population who see themselves sidelined by the elites and passed over in favor of minorities," 5.
123. Chappelle, *Age of Spin*, 35:00.
124. Volf, *Exclusion and Embrace*, 103.
125. Williams, *Resurrection*, 7.
126. Bradley, *Liberating Black Theology*, 79.
127. Bradley, *Liberating Black Theology*, 52.
128. Williams, *Resurrection*, 9.
129. Dostoyevsky, *Brothers Karamazov*, 320.
130. Dostoyevsky, *Brothers Karamazov*, 164.
131. Dostoyevsky, *Brothers Karamazov*, 319.
132. Dostoyevsky, *Brothers Karamazov*, 321.
133. Dostoyevsky, *Brothers Karamazov*, 321.
134. Taylor, *Sources of the Self*, 452.
135. Volf, *Exclusion and Embrace*, 119.

136. Williams, *Dostoyevsky*, 153.
137. Williams, *Way of St Benedict*, 18.
138. Williams, *Way of St Benedict*, 15.
139. Williams, *Way of St Benedict*, 32.
140. Peggy Noonan, quoted in Sacks, *Morality*, 4.
141. As recounted by Will Willimon on "Episode 322: The God Fathers of Crackers," 25:00.

CHAPTER SIX

142. Brueggemann, *Prophetic Imagination*, 1–19.
143. Brueggemann, *Prophetic Imagination*, 3.
144. Gutiérrez, *Theology of Liberation*, xxxviii.
145. Felski, *Limits of Critique*, 87–88.
146. Oswalt, *Book of Isaiah*, 630.
147. Brueggemann, *Prophetic Imagination*, xii.
148. Brueggemann, *Prophetic Imagination*, 46.
149. Brueggemann, *Prophetic Imagination*, 81.
150. Brueggemann, *Prophetic Imagination*, 116.
151. Brueggemann, *Prophetic Imagination*, 52.
152. Brueggemann, *Prophetic Imagination*, 95.
153. Brueggemann, *Prophetic Imagination*, 99.
154. Hauerwas, *In Conversation*, 92.
155. Google "SNL More Cowbell skit."
156. Gutiérrez, *Theology of Liberation*, xxiii.
157. McCaulley, *Reading While Black*, 5–13.
158. Berry, *Need to Be Whole*, 176.
159. Barack Obama, quoted in Sacks, *Morality*, 183.
160. Volf and Croasmun, *For the Life of the World*, 55.
161. David Burrell, quoted in Hauerwas, *Peaceable Kingdom*, 150.
162. Cone, *Cross and the Lynching Tree*, 165–66.

CHAPTER SEVEN

163. For example, see the relevant data from the General Social Survey, summarized well in Burge, "Nondenominational Churches Are Adding Millions of Members. Where Are They Coming From?"
164. Taylor, *Secular Age*, 624.
165. I feel indebted to cite Scot McKnight here because I've heard him say something along these lines.
166. Scott, *Two Cheers for Anarchism*, xii.
167. Watkin, *Thinking Through Creation*, 28.
168. Gail Godwin, quoted in Brueggemann, *First and Second Samuel*, 7.
169. Quoted in Haidt, *Righteous Mind*, 331.
170. Haidt, *Righteous Mind*, 332–333.

171. In context, Paul is speaking of the diversity of spiritual gifts God gives people, though it seems fair to suggest this might apply to more than just spiritual gifts.
172. Bulgakov, *Sophiology of Death*, 32.
173. Taylor, *Sources of the Self*, 401.
174. Bradley, "White racism is not the cause."
175. See the section "How politics makes smart people stupid," in Klein, *Why We're Polarized*, 90–98.
176. Bulgakov, *Sophiology of Death*, 33.
177. Bulgakov, *Sophiology of Death*, 39.
178. Crawford, *World Beyond Your Head*, 236.

CHAPTER EIGHT

179. Florer-Bixler, *How to Have an Enemy*, 34.
180. Florer-Bixler, *How to Have an Enemy*, 34.
181. Berry, *The Need to Be Whole*, 406–7.
182. Florer-Bixler, *How to Have an Enemy*, 132.
183. Berry, *Need to Be Whole*, 189–90.
184. Berry, *Need to Be Whole*, 15.
185. Florer-Bixler, *How to Have an Enemy*, 172.
186. Florer-Bixler, *How to Have an Enemy*, 176.
187. Florer-Bixler, *How to Have an Enemy*, 180.
188. Beltran, "To Understand Trump's Support," para. 5.
189. Toni Morrison's *The Bluest Eye* employs an elegant and moving portrayal of this. James W. Loewen's *The Mississippi Culture* was one of the first academic employments of the trope, upon which many have subsequently built.
190. Berry, *Need to Be Whole*, 348.
191. Tran, *Asian Americans and the Spirit*, 69.
192. Tran, *Asian Americans and the Spirit*, 6–7.
193. Tran, *Asian Americans and the Spirit*, 13.
194. Tran, *Asian Americans and the Spirit*, 127–35.
195. Tran, *Asian Americans and the Spirit*, 13.
196. Emerson and Smith, *Divided by Faith*, 76–91.
197. Florer-Bixler, *How to Have an Enemy*, 25.
198. Florer-Bixler, *How to Have an Enemy*, 27.
199. Florer-Bixler, *How to Have an Enemy*, 28.
200. Berry, *Need to Be Whole*, 349.
201. Berry, *Need to Be Whole*, 111.
202. Berry, *Need to Be Whole*, 20.
203. Florer-Bixler, *How to Have an Enemy*, 16.
204. Berry, *Need to Be Whole*, 454.
205. Berry, *Need to Be Whole*, 454.
206. Berry, *Need to Be Whole*, 455.
207. McWhorter, "'Racism' Has Too Many Definitions," para. 8.
208. Berry, *Need to Be Whole*, 35.
209. "How Informed Are Americans," 1.
210. Murray, *Madness of Crowds*, 232.

211. Jennings, "My Anger, God's Righteous Indignation," starting at para. 19.
212. Berry, *Need to Be Whole*, 234.
213. Berry, *Need to Be Whole*, 234–35.
214. Florer-Bixler, *How to Have an Enemy*, 64.
215. Berry, *Need to Be Whole*, 24.
216. Berry, *Need to Be Whole*, 333.
217. Berry, *Need to Be Whole*, 3.
218. Berry, *Need to Be Whole*, 134–35.
219. Florer-Bixler, *How to Have an Enemy*, 16.
220. Berry, *Need to Be Whole*, 408.
221. Farhad Manjoo, quoted in Berry, *Need to Be Whole*, 415–16.

CHAPTER NINE

222. Rom 9:1–15; Rom 11:1; Phil 3:5–6.
223. McKnight, *Reading Romans Backwards*, 21.
224. McKnight, *Reading Romans Backwards*, 103.
225. Dunn, *New Perspective on Paul*, 219.
226. Barth, *Church Dogmatics* IV:1, 233–34.
227. Volf, *Exclusion and Embrace*, 271.
228. Yoder, *Politics of Jesus*, 130–31.
229. Van Zant quoted in Taysom, "Why Neil Young and Lynyrd Skynyrd were locked in a long-running feud," para. 7.
230. Neil Young, quoted in Green, "Flashback: Neil Young Covers 'Sweet Home Alabama' in 1977," para. 4.

Bibliography

Barth, Karl. *Church Dogmatics*. Vol. 4:1. Edinburgh: T. & T. Clark, 1961.
Beaton, Caroline. "Why Millennials are Lonely." *Forbes* (February 9, 2017). https://www.forbes.com/sites/carolinebeaton/2017/02/09/why-millennials-are-lonely/?sh=4f23e4c37c35.
Beltran, Cristina. "To Understand Trump's Support, We Must Think in Terms of Multiracial Whiteness." *Washington Post* (January 15, 2021). https://www.washingtonpost.com/opinions/2021/01/15/understand-trumps-support-we-must-think-terms-multiracial-whiteness/.
Berry, Wendell. *The Need to Be Whole: Patriotism and the History of Prejudice*. Berkeley: Shoemaker & Company, 2022.
———. *The World-Ending Fire: The Essential Wendell Berry*. Berkeley: Counterpoint, 2017.
Bishop, Bill. *The Big Sort: Why the Clustering of Like-Minded America is Tearing Us Apart*. New York: Mariner, 2009.
Blythe, Will. *To Hate Like This Is to Be Happy Forever: A Thoroughly Obsessive, Intermittently Uplifting, and Occasionally Unbiased Account of the Duke–North Carolina Basketball Rivalry*. New York: Harper, 2007.
Boulton, Matthew Myers. *Life in God: John Calvin, Practical Formation, and the Future of Protestant Theology*. Grand Rapids: Zondervan, 2011.
Bradley, Anthony B. *Liberating Black Theology: The Bible and the Black Experience in America*. Wheaton, IL: Crossway, 2010.
———. (@drantbradley). "White racism is not the cause of *everything* that's wrong in poor black communities across America. Progressives ignore this fact, infantilize blackness, & won't invite moral responsibility and conservatives know this but tend to weaponize it for their own self-righteousness." *Twitter* (April 21, 2021, 11:02 PM). https://twitter.com/drantbradley/status/1385081480506974211.
Bregman, Rutger. *Utopia for Realists: How We Can Build the Ideal World*. Boston: Little, Brown, and Company, 2017.
Brown, Brené. *Braving the Wilderness*. New York: Random House, 2017.
Brueggemann, Walter. *First and Second Samuel*. Interpretation: A Bible Commentary for Teaching and Preaching. Louisville: John Knox, 1990.
———. *Genesis*. Interpretation: A Bible Commentary for Teaching and Preaching. Atlanta: John Knox, 1982.

Bibliography

———. *The Prophetic Imagination*. 2nd ed. Minneapolis: Fortress, 2001.

Bulgakov, Sergius. *The Sophiology of Death: Essays on Eschatology: Personal, Political, Universal*. Translated by Roberto J. De La Noval. Eugene, OR: Cascade, 2021.

Burge, Ryan P. "Nondenominational Churches Are Adding Millions of Members. Where Are They Coming From?" *Christianity Today*, August 5, 2022. www.christianitytoday.com/news/2022/august/nondenominational-growth-mainline-protestant-decline-survey.html.

Busch, Eberhard. *Karl Barth: His Life from Letters and Autobiographical Texts*. Translated by John Bowden. Philadelphia: Fortress, 1976.

Campbell, Bradley, and Jason Manning. *The Rise of Victimhood Culture: Microaggressions, Safe Spaces, and the New Culture Wars*. London: Palgrave Macmillan, 2018.

"Census Bureau Releases New Estimates on America's Families and Living Arrangements." https://www.census.gov/newsroom/press-releases/2021/families-and-living-arrangements.html.

Chappelle, Dave. *The Age of Spin: Dave Chappelle Live at The Hollywood Palladium*. Netflix, 35:00.

Cone, James. *The Cross and the Lynching Tree*. Maryknoll, NY: Orbis, 2015.

———. *For My People: Black Theology and the Black Church*. Maryknoll, NY: Orbis, 1996.

Crawford, Matthew B. *The World Beyond Your Head: On Becoming an Individual in an Age of Distraction*. New York: Farrar, Straus and Giroux, 2015.

Dostoyevsky, Fyodor. *The Brothers Karamazov*. Translated by Richard Pevear and Larissa Volokhonsky. New York: Alfred A. Knopf, 1992.

Dunn, James. *The New Perspective on Paul*. Rev. ed. Grand Rapids: Eerdmans, 2008.

Emerson, Michael O., and Christian Smith. *Divided by Faith: Evangelical Religion and the Problem of Race in America*. New York: Oxford University Press, 2000.

"Episode 322: The God Fathers of Crackers." *Crackers and Grape Juice*, September 11, 2021, podcast, 25:00, https://crackersandgrapejuice.com/episode-322-the-god-fathers-of-crackers/.

Felski, Rita. *The Limits of Critique*. Chicago: University of Chicago Press, 2015.

Florer-Bixler, Melissa. *How to Have an Enemy: Righteous Anger & the Work of Peace*. Harrisonburg, VA: Herald, 2021.

Green, Andy. "Flashback: Neil Young Covers 'Sweet Home Alabama' in 1977." *Rolling Stone* (January 25, 2015). https://www.rollingstone.com/music/music-news/flashback-neil-young-covers-sweet-home-alabama-in-1977-186638/.

Gutiérrez, Gustavo. *A Theology of Liberation: History, Politics, and Salvation*. Translated and edited by Sister Caridad Inda and John Eagleson. Maryknoll, NY: Orbis, 2010.

Haidt, Jonathan. *The Righteous Mind: Why Good People Are Divided by Politics and Religion*. New York: Vintage, 2012.

Harari, Yuval Noah. *Homo Deus: A Brief History of Tomorrow*. New York: Harper Perennial, 2017.

Hart, David Bentley. *Theological Territories: A David Bentley Hart Digest*. Notre Dame: University of Notre Dame Press, 2020.

Hauerwas, Stanley. *After Christendom: How the Church is to Behave if Freedom, Justice, and a Christian Nation are Bad Ideas*. Nashville: Abingdon, 1991.

———. *In Conversation: Samuel Wells and Stanley Hauerwas*. Facilitated by Maureen Knudsen Langdoc. New York: Church Publishing, 2020.

———. *The Peaceable Kingdom*. Notre Dame: University of Notre Dame Press, 1983.

———. *The Work of Theology*. Grand Rapids: Eerdmans, 2015.

Bibliography

Heath, Joseph. *Enlightenment 2.0: Restoring Sanity to Our Politics, Our Economy, and Our Lives.* Toronto: Harper Perennial, 2015.

hooks, bell. *Outlaw Culture.* New York: Rutledge Classics, 2006.

"How Informed are Americans about Race and Policing?" *Skeptic.* https://www.skeptic.com/research-center/reports/Research-Report-CUPES-007.pdf

Iyengar, Shanto, and Sean J. Westwood. "Fear and Loathing across Party Lines: New Evidence of Group Polarization." *American Journal of Political Science* 59.3 (July 2015) 690–707.

Jennings, Willie James. *After Whiteness: An Education in Belonging.* Grand Rapids: Eerdmans, 2020.

———. *The Christian Imagination: Theology and the Origins of Race.* New Haven: Yale University Press, 2010.

———. "My Anger, God's Righteous Indignation." https://faith.yale.edu/media/my-anger-gods-righteous-indignation.

King, Martin Luther, Jr. "Letter from Birmingham Jail." https://www.africa.upenn.edu/Articles_Gen/Letter_Birmingham.html.

Klein, Ezra. *Why We're Polarized.* New York: Avid Reader, 2020.

Klein, Ezra, and Alvin Chang. "Political Identity Is Fair Game for Hatred: How Republicans and Democrats Discriminate." *Vox* (December 7, 2015). https://www.vox.com/2015/12/7/9790764/partisan-discrimination.

Lohfink, Gerhard. *Does God Need the Church?: Toward a Theology of the People of God.* Translated by Linda M. Maloney. Collegeville, MN: Liturgical, 1999.

Leithart, Peter J. "Clashing Victimocracies." *First Things* (November 2, 2018). https://www.firstthings.com/web-exclusives/2018/11/clashing-victimocracies.

———. *The End of Protestantism: Pursuing Unity in a Fragmented Church.* Grand Rapids: Brazos, 2016.

McCaulley, Esau. *Reading While Black: African American Biblical Interpretation as an Exercise in Hope.* Downer's Grove, IL: InterVarsity, 2020.

McKnight, Scot. *Reading Romans Backwards: A Gospel of Peace in the Midst of Empire.* Waco, TX: Baylor University Press, 2019.

McWhorter, John. "'Racism' Has Too Many Definitions. We Need Another Term." *The New York Times* (May 17, 2022). https://www.nytimes.com/2022/05/17/opinion/buffalo-racism.html/

Minogue, Kenneth. *The Liberal Mind.* Indianapolis: Liberty Fund, 2000.

Murray, Douglas. *The Madness of Crowds: Gender, Race, and Identity.* London: Bloomsbury, 2019.

Obama, Barack. "How to Make this Moment the Turning Point for Real Change." https://barackobama.medium.com/how-to-make-this-moment-the-turning-point-for-real-change-9fa209806067.

Oswalt, John N. *The Book of Isaiah: Chapters 40–66.* The New International Commentary on the Old Testament. Grand Rapids: Eerdmans, 1998.

Parker, Priya. "Episode 389: How to Make Meetings Less Terrible." *Freakonomics Podcast*, September 18, 2019, podcast, 34:21, https://freakonomics.com/podcast/how-to-make-meetings-less-terrible-ep-389/.

Pluckrose, Helen, and James Lindsay. *Cynical Theories: How Activist Scholarship Made Everything about Race, Gender, and Identity—and Why This Harms Everybody.* Durham, NC: Pitchstone, 2020.

Bibliography

Rogan, Joe. "Joe Rogan Experience #1595—Ira Glasser." *The Joe Rogan Experience*, January 15, 2021, podcast, 63:00. https://www.jrepodcast.com/episode/joe-rogan-experience-1595-ira-glasser/.

Rutledge, Fleming. *The Crucifixion: Understanding the Death of Jesus Christ*. Grand Rapids: Eerdmans, 2015.

Ryan, Christopher. *Civilized to Death: The Price of Progress*. New York: Avid Reader, 2019.

Sacks, Jonathan. *Morality: Restoring the Common Good in Divided Times*. New York: Basic, 2020.

Scott, James C. *Two Cheers for Anarchism: Six Easy Pieces on Autonomy, Dignity, and Meaningful Work and Play*. Princeton, NJ: Princeton University Press, 2012.

Singal, Jesse. *The Quick Fix: Why Fad Psychology Can't Cure Our Social Ills*. New York: Farrar, Straus and Giroux, 2021.

Simmons, Bill. "Sarah Silverman on 'Funny' in 2019, Cancel Culture, 'Big Mouth,' Death Threats, the 2020 Election, and 'Big Little Lies.'" *Bill Simmons Podcast*, August 8, 2019, podcast, 10:45, https://www.theringer.com/the-bill-simmons-podcast/2019/8/8/20798119/sarah-silverman-funny-2019-cancel-culture-big-mouth-death-threats-the-2020-election-big-little-lies.

Smiley, Tavis. "The One Single Thing Donald Trump and Martin Luther King, Jr. Have In Common." *Time* (December 1, 2017). https://time.com/5042070/donald-trump-martin-luther-king-mlk/.

Solzhenitsyn, Aleksandr. *The Gulag Archipelago 1918–56*. Translated by Thomas P. Whitney and Harry Willets. London: Harvill, 2003.

Taylor, Charles. *A Secular Age*. Reprinted ed. Cambridge: Belknap Press of Harvard University Press, 2018.

———. *Sources of the Self: The Making of Modern Identity*. Cambridge: Harvard University Press, 1989.

Taysom, Joe. "Why Neil Young and Lynyrd Skynyrd were locked in a long-running feud." *Far Out Magazine* (June 20, 2021). https://faroutmagazine.co.uk/neil-young-lynyrd-skynyrd-feud-sweet-home-alabama-battle/.

Teresa, Mother. "Acceptance Speech." https://www.nobelprize.org/prizes/peace/1979/teresa/26200-mother-teresa-acceptance-speech-1979/.

Tolentino, Jia. *Trick Mirror: Reflections on Self-Delusion*. New York: Random House, 2019.

Tran, Jonathan. *Asian Americans and the Spirit of Racial Capitalism*. New York: Oxford University Press, 2022.

"2020 Democratic Party presidential primaries." *Wikipedia*, https://en.wikipedia.org/wiki/2020_Democratic_Party_presidential_primaries.

Vavreck, Lynn. "A Measure of Identity: Are You Wedded to Your Party?" *The New York Times* (January 30, 2017). https://www.nytimes.com/2017/01/31/upshot/are-you-married-to-your-party.html.

Volf, Miroslav. *Exclusion and Embrace: A Theological Exploration of Identity, Otherness, and Reconciliation*. Nashville: Abingdon, 1996.

Volf, Miroslav, and Matthew Croasmun. *For the Life of the World: Theology That Makes a Difference*. Grand Rapids: Brazos, 2019.

Wasserman, David. "Purple America Has All But Disappeared." *FiveThirtyEight* (March 8, 2017). https://fivethirtyeight.com/features/purple-america-has-all-but-disappeared/.

Watkin, Christopher. *Thinking Through Creation: Genesis 1 and 2 as Tools of Cultural Critique*. Phillipsburg, NJ: P&R, 2017.

Watts, Jon, dir. *Spider-Man: Far From Home*. Columbia Pictures and Marvel Studios, 2019.

West, Geoffrey. *Scale: The Universal Laws of Life, Growth, and Death in Organisms, Cities, and Companies.* New York: Penguin, 2018.
Williams, Rowan. *Dostoyevsky: Language, Faith, and Fiction.* Waco, TX: Baylor University Press, 2011.
———. *Looking East in Winter: Contemporary Thought and the Eastern Christian Tradition.* London: Bloomsbury Continuum, 2021.
———. *Resurrection: Interpreting the Easter Gospel.* London: Darton, Longman and Todd, 2014.
———. *The Way of St Benedict.* London: Bloomsbury, 2020.
Yoder, John Howard. *The Politics of Jesus.* 2nd ed. Grand Rapids: Eerdmans, 1994.
———. *The War of the Lamb: The Ethics of Nonviolence and Peacemaking.* Grand Rapids: Brazos, 2009.

Made in United States
Troutdale, OR
05/17/2024